Y0-AIO-804

FROM RADICAL LEFT TO EXTREME RIGHT

Current Periodicals of Protest,
Controversy, or Dissent-U.S.A.

A Bibliography Containing Dispassionate Summaries of Content Samples to Guide Librarians and Other Educators Through the Polemic Fringe

ROBERT H. MULLER
Editor

1967

Third Printing - July, 1968

Campus Publishers
711 NORTH UNIVERSITY AVE.
ANN ARBOR, MICHIGAN 48108

© 1967 Robert H. Muller

Library of Congress
Catalog Card Number 67-29985

*Ref
Z
7165
.U5
M8*

3rd Printing, July 1968, includes two supplements: (1) Changes up to August 1, 1967; (2) Errata.

Lithoprinted in the U. S. A.

TABLE OF CONTENTS

Quotations   viii
Preface   xi
Unverified Titles   xix

Chapter 1 - Civil Rights and Negro

*CORE-lator (Congress of Racial Equality)	1
Crisis (NAACP)	1
Freedomways (Negro Freedom Movement)	2
Interracial Review (Catholic Interracial Council of New York)	3
Liberator ("Afro-American protest movement")	4
Movement (Student Nonviolent Coordinating Committee)	5
Muhammad Speaks (Black Muslim)	6
New South (Southern Regional Council)	7
Petal Paper	9
*SCLC Newsletter (Southern Christian Leadership Conference)	9
Southern Courier	10
Southern Patriot (Southern Conference Educational Fund)	11
*The Voice (Student Nonviolent Coordinating Committee)	11
WCLC Newsletter (Western Christian Leadership Conference)	12

Chapter 2 - Left of Center

Activist	13
ADA Legislative Newsletter (Americans for Democratic Action)	14
ADA World (Americans for Democratic Action)	15
American Dialog	15
*American Socialist (American Socialist Organizing Committee)	16
American-Soviet Facts (see Facts)	24
*Antithesis (Marxism-Leninism)	17
Bulletin of International Socialism (American Committee for the 4th International)	19
Catholic Worker (Catholic Worker Movement)	20
Challenge-Desafio (Progressive Labor Party)	21
Despite Everything	22
Dissent (Socialist)	23
Facts (National Council of American-Soviet Friendship)	24
*Free Student (Started by May 2nd Movement)	25
*Frontier (Merged with The Nation)	26
Hammer and Steel Newsletter (Marxist-Leninist)	27
I. F. Stone's Weekly	28
Industrial Worker (Industrial Workers of the World)	29
*Insurgent (Du Bois Clubs of America)	29
International Socialist Review (Socialist Workers' Party)	30
Liberation	31

*Have ceased publication, June 1968.

The Militant (Socialist Workers' Party)	32
Monthly Review (Independent Socialist)	34
National Guardian (Name changed to <u>Guardian</u>)	35
New America (Socialist Party)	37
New Politics ("A Journal of Socialist Thought")	39
New World Review	40
News and Letters	42
Partisan (Youth Against War and Fascism)	43
People's World	43
Political Affairs (Communist Party, U.S.A.)	44
Progressive	46
Progressive Labor (Progressive Labor Party)	47
SDS Bulletin (Students for a Democratic Society)	48
Spark-Chispa (Progressive Labor Party, West Coast)	48
Spartacist (Dissidents from the Socialist Workers' Party)	49
Studies on the Left	50
Viet-Report	51
Weekly People (Socialist Labor Party)	53
Western Socialist (World Socialist Party of the U.S. and Canada)	54
The Worker (Communist Party, U.S.A.)	55
Worker's World (Worker's World Party)	56
Young Socialist (Young Socialist Alliance)	56

Chapter 3 - Miscellaneous

Age of Reason (Freethinkers of America)	58
*American Atheist: A Voice of Reason (Freethought Society of America)	58
Between the Lines (Charles A. Wells)	59
Capsule News (Morris Beale)	60
Church and State (Protestants and other Americans United for Separation of Church and State)	61
Civil Liberties (American Civil Liberties Union)	62
Destiny	63
FCNL Washington Newsletter (Friends Committee on National Legislation)	64
Federalist (United World Federalists)	64
The Independent	65
Intercollegiate Review: A Review of Scholarship and Opinion	67
Left and Right	68
Minority of One	69
New Leader (American Labor Conference of International Affairs)	71
New University Thought	72
Ramparts	73
Realist	74

*Have ceased publication, June 1968.

Rights (Emergency Civil Liberties Committee)	75
Social Questions Bulletin (Methodist Federation for Social Action)	76
*Towards Anarchism	77
World News and Comments (now William Winter Comments)	78

Chapter 4 - Pacifist

*CNVA Bulletin (Committee for Nonviolent Action)	80
Fellowship (Fellowship of Reconciliation)	80
Four Lights (U.S. Section of Women's International League for Peace and Freedom)	82
News Notes (Central Committee for Conscientious Objectors)	82
Peace (American Pax Association)	83
Peace Action (Voice of Peace from the Nation's Capital)	84
Peacemaker (Peacemaker Movement)	84
Reporter for Conscience' Sake (National Service Board for Religious Objectors)	85
Sane World (National Committee for a Sane Nuclear Policy)	86
*Student Peace Union Bulletin	86
War/Peace Report	87
WRL News (War Resister's League)	88

Chapter 5 - Race-Oriented

The Citizen (Citizen's Council of America)	90
Common Sense	91
Councilor	92
Cross and Flag (Christian Nationalist Crusade)	93
National Christian News	94
National Chronicle	95
National Renaissance Bulletin (National Renaissance Party)	96
Pilgrim Torch (Soldiers of the Cross)	97
*Rockwell Report (American Nazi Party)	97
Stormtrooper (American Nazi Party)	98
Thunderbolt (National States Rights Party)	98
Truth Seeker	99
The White American (National White Americans Party)	99

Chapter 6 - Right of Center

American Flag Committee Newsletter (American Flag Committee)	101
American Mercury	102
American Opinion (John Birch Society)	103
America's Future (America's Future, Inc.)	104
The Capital Voice (Dale Crowley)	105
Christian Anti-Communist Crusade Newsletter (Christian Anti-Communist Crusade)	106

*Have ceased publication, June 1968.

Christian Beacon (Bible Presbyterian Church)	107
Christian Crusade (Billy James Hargis)	107
Christian Economics	108
Dan Smoot Report	110
Dart Bulletin (Paul Dickson)	111
Economic Council Letter (National Economic Council)	112
Fact Finder	112
Facts For Freedom (see In a Nutshell)	122
Firing Line (American Legion)	113
Free Enterprise	115
Freedom's Facts (All American Conference)	113
Freedom Talks (see Life Lines)	128
Freedom's Way	114
Freeman (Foundation for Economic Education)	115
Gospel Truth (Southwest Radio Church of the Air)	116
Grass Roots	117
Greater Nebraskan (Congress of Freedom)	118
Heads Up (Karl Prussion)	119
Herald of Freedom (Frank A. Capell)	120
Human Events	120
IMUA Spotlight (Hawaii Foundation for American Freedoms, Inc.)	121
In a Nutshell	122
Independent American (Free Men Speak)	123
Inform-National Reports	124
Kansas Free Lance (Mr. and Mrs. Dwight Payton)	125
Keeping the Record Straight (Edith Essig)	126
Liberty Letter (Liberty Lobby)	127
Life Lines (Melvin Munn)	128
Manion Forum (Clarence Manion)	129
Mindszenty Report (Cardinal Mindszenty Foundation)	130
Minute Women (Minute Women of the U.S.A.)	130
Modern Age (Foundation for Foreign Affairs)	131
*National Forecast (National Forecast Ministry, Inc.)	132
National Program Letter (National Education Program)	133
New Guard (Young Americans for Freedom)	133
New Individualist Review (J. M. Cobb)	134
News and Views (National Layman's Council of the Church League of America)	136
Objectivist (Ayn Rand and Nathaniel Branden)	136
On Target (Minute Men)	138
Our American Heritage Committee News Bulletin (Our American Heritage Committee)	139
The Plain Truth (Ambassador College)	140
Rampart Journal of Individualistic Thought	141

*Have ceased publication, June 1968.

Rank and File (Conservative employee magazine)	142
Review of the News (John Birch Society)	143
Richard Cotten's Conservative Viewpoint	144
SOS!!! U.S.A. Ship of State (Anti-Communist Confederation of Polish Freedom Fighters in U.S.A.)	145
Tactics (Anti-Communist Liaison)	146
Task Force (Defenders of the American Constitution)	147
*Tocsin	148
Top of the News (Fulton Lewis, Jr.)	149
The Truth About Communism (Political Science Club, Marquette University High School)	150
The Wanderer (Catholic, Independent)	150
Washington Observer Newsletter (see American Mercury)	102
Weekly Crusader	151
Wire Magazine	152
Woman Constitutionalist (Women for Constitutional Government)	153
Alphabetical list of titles	155

SUPPLEMENT No. 1. Updating information to August 1, 1967. Most of the changes occurred in address, frequency of publication, circulation, price of subscription, and format. 158

SUPPLEMENT No. 2. Primarily errata - corrections of minor spelling and typographical errors. 164

*Have ceased publication, June 1968.

The true believer is everywhere on the march, and both by converting and antagonizing he is shaping the world in his own image. And whether we line up with him or against him, it is well that we should know all we can concerning his nature and potentialities.

      Eric Hoffer

The genuine man of words delights in the clash of thought and in the give-and-take of controversy . . . . His vanity, it is true, often prompts him to defend his speculations with savagery and even venom; but his appeal is usually to reason and not to faith.

      Eric Hoffer

Whenever there is the war of ideas, every tongue takes a side. There is no neutrality. Even silence is no neutrality . . . .

      Wendell Phillips

. . . The First Amendment (of the U.S. Constitution) allows all ideas to be expressed--whether orthodox, popular, off-beat, or repulsive . . . . People are left to pick and choose between competing offerings. . . .

      Justice William O. Douglass

The real problem of the First Amendment comes when the speaker is expressing ideas we hate or fear or is speaking in the hope of destroying the freedom of others.

      Martin Shapiro

To allow opposition by speech seems to indicate that you think the speech impotent, as when a man says that he has squared the circle, or that you do not care wholeheartedly for the result, or that you doubt either your power or your premises. But when men have realized that time has upset many fighting faiths, they may come to believe even more than they believe the very foundations of their conduct that the ultimate good desired is better reached by free trade in ideas--that the best test of truth is the power of the thought to get itself accepted in the competition of the market . . . . We should be eternally vigilant against attempts to check the expression of opinions that we loathe and believe to be fraught with death, unless they so imminently threaten immediate interference with the lawful and pressing purposes of the law that an immediate check is required to save the country.

Justice Oliver Wendell Holmes

A function of free speech under our system of government is to invite dispute. It may indeed best serve its high purpose when it induces a condition of unrest, creates dissatisfaction with conditions as they are, or even stirs people to anger. Speech is often provocative and challenging. It may strike at prejudices and preconceptions and have profound unsettling effects as it presses for acceptance of an idea . . . .

Justice Potter Stewart

The real value of freedom of speech is not to the minority that wants to talk, but to the majority that does not want to listen.

Zechariah Chafee

One of the basic policies which should govern the services of all libraries: There should be the fullest practicable provision of material presenting all points of view concerning the problems and issues of our times, international, national, and local . . . .

From the "Library Bill of Rights"
Adopted by the Council of the American Library Association

If democracy is to survive, there must always be dissent. There must always be the taboo-breaker. There must always be the struggle for the complete freedom for all men to think as they wish, to speak as they wish, to write as they wish."

Lyle Stuart

Preface

The "Library Bill of Rights" commits librarians to a policy of providing materials presenting all points of view concerning the problems and issues of our times. How seriously such responsibility is taken depends on a number of factors. Some libraries limit themselves to providing books and periodicals that historically summarize the problems and issues of our times. Others feel that one must go further and make available the actual current first-hand communications from the propagandists themselves. Quite a few libraries minimize the importance of controversial materials in order to make the library invulnerable to attack or to avoid offense. Others limit provision to materials of quality and exclude those publications that are poorly written, unsupported by facts, offensive, crude, excessively militant, etc. More often than not, however, the actual reason for neglecting certain types of publication is not deliberate effort at exclusion but the plain difficulty of becoming aware of fringe publications and how to obtain them.

As educators, librarians have a responsibility to ensure that the public has an opportunity to be informed about all manner of ideas advocated, no matter how obnoxious they may be to some of us. How uninformed the public is was demonstrated in November 1965 when the Communist Party went on trial for the second time for failing to register as an agent of the Soviet Union. The eight men and four women picked to hear the case before Judge William B. Jones in the U.S. District Court of Washington, D.C., swore: they had not read, seen, nor heard anything derogatory about the Communist Party, and; had never read books or articles by such conservative or rightist authors as Elizabeth Bentley, Whittaker Chambers, Louis Budenz, J. B. Mathews, Herbert Philbrick, William F. Buckley Jr., Gerald L. K. Smith, Westbrook Pegler, Dan Smoot, Robert Welch, Dr. Fred Schwarz, or Dr. George George Benson; nor listened to radio programs conducted by Fulton Lewis Jr., John T. Flynn, "Life Line," "Facts Forum," "Clarence Manion Forum," or the 20th Century Reformation Hour."

With rare exceptions, college and public libraries tend to shy away from the highly controversial in their subscriptions to periodicals. They often limit themselves to what is included in collective indexes, to magazines of culture and quality, to mass-circulation periodicals, and to a few titles of an extremist nature that are donated by pressure groups.

The following quotation is probably quite accurate in its characterization of public library policy:

> The public librarian's duty is to encourage the democratic dialogue. Unfortunately . . . the public library is committed to ideological neutrality . . . . All the means of communication--newspapers, popular magazines, radio, and television--are in essential agreement with each other. It is my contention that the ideological neutrality of the public library merely reinforces mass thinking. If you want to confirm this suspicion, check the periodicals displayed at the local branch of your public library. The list, with few exceptions, parallels the magazines for sale at your favorite grocery store. . . .[1]

The Assistant Editor of the Library Journal conducted a survey in 1964 in which he sent a list of 21 magazines to 120 public libraries (of which 100 responded) to determine the extent to which extremist publications were received and made available to the public. He found a widespread lack of representation and concluded that, "public libraries in the United States continue, very cautiously, to cling to the middle of the road."[2] He also advocated that it is "incumbent upon librarians, not only to provide dissenting views, but to educate the public to the existence of these views wherever they are available."[3] He felt that librarians ought not sit back and wait until specific titles are demanded by segments of the public. The compiler agrees with this activist philosophy of librarianship whereby a deliberate effort is made to provide within the library a forum for dissenting voices appearing in print. The difficulty is that librarians often do not know enough about the nature of these dissenting voices and the sources for obtaining them. This compilation is a preliminary effort to fill this gap of knowledge.

The compilation is primarily designed to provide information to librarians to help them in the task of selection, so that they can proceed, as they see fit, to create an awareness by the public of the existence of propagandistic or polemic periodicals expressing dissident, opposition, or minority opinion. Although this compilation is limited to periodicals, it should be noted that much polemic material is also published in other forms--pamphlets, paperbacks, books, etc.

[1] Otto Kirchner-Dean, "Book Selection and the Democratic Process," Library Journal, XCI (June 1, 1966), 2765.
[2] John H. Berry, "Demand for Dissent," Library Journal, XV (October 15, 1964), 3917.
[3] Ibid., p. 3914.

Excluded from this listing were those periodical titles that seemed to be fairly widely known or well established, such as the liberal Nation and the New Republic and the conservative National Review and U.S. News and World Report. The emphasis was placed on publications that were judged to be "radical" and polemic, or that had a definite bias or orientation toward expressing opposition, dissent, disagreement, or divergence from the mainstream of opinion. It was not always easy to make this determination consistently, especially since many fringe groups or individuals regard themselves to be in the mainstream. The inclusion or exclusion of some titles may well be questioned, for instance, those that are only mildly conservative or liberal.

The first step in our effort was to identify the titles currently being published. This first step was not an easy one since available published directories were incomplete, partly out of date, or not wholly applicable. For instance The First National Directory of "Rightist" Groups, Publications and Some Individuals in the United States (and Some Foreign Countries), 5th ed., 1965, published by Alert Americans Association, contained 3,406 entries, of which over 80% were not related to periodicals and in which periodical entries were not easily identifiable. The Directory: America's Most Controversial Periodicals, published by USA Guidelines Publications 1965, contained 140 titles, some of which were not really controversial in nature and others of which were no longer published. The Agcomm Directory One listed 95 titles of interest to "libertarians." Although a few new titles were gleaned from the latter list, it also contained much that fell outside the controversial or polemic. Help was also obtained from the Labadie Collection of The University of Michigan, which receives, for purposes of preservation and research, many periodicals of the radical Left and the extreme Right. The Curator of the Labadie Collection was helpful in the winnowing and selection process. For titles not subscribed to by The University of Michigan (and there were over 40 of these), it was necessary to obtain sample copies from the publishers, which was not always an easy task.

The second step was to provide certain routine information, i.e., address, frequency, circulation (when obtainable), subscription price, the birth year or origin of publication, and its format.

The third step was to prepare a meaningful description of the content of the periodical: To do so, it was decided to take three issues (more when readily obtainable) and to have an unbiased and dispassionate summary prepared by students employed on an hourly basis; the abstractors were paid for in part out of a grant to the compiler from the Jackson Social Welfare Fund, of the First Unitarian Church of Ann Arbor. (This fund is set up to support projects related to the advancement of "the understanding and acceptance of the great principles of the First Amendment of the Constitution of the United States.") The quality of the summaries prepared by the student assistants varied, of course, depending on a number of factors. Editing and rewriting was necessary to improve the language and also to eliminate any bias that might have inadvertently crept in.

It was assumed that a close look at three issues would be sufficient to give an abstractor a reliable impression of the general character and editorial policy of a given periodical. This assumption was based on the observation that a periodical usually does not change sufficiently in character over a span of several years to invalidate the impression of its editorial policy gained from a sample of three issues. A periodical may deal with different specific subject matter from year to year; but, if it expects to hold its subscribers or readers, it can not risk too wide a deviation from the policy position that is evident in even a small sample. Most people tend to subscribe to periodicals that reinforce their predispositions; hence a periodical must be fairly consistent from issue to issue in fulfilling its readers' expectations with regard to biases, militancy, targets of aggression, aims, ideals, fears, and hopes.

The reason for preparing summaries of the actual content was that we aimed to avoid the kind of annotation that was too general to be meaningful and failed to get down to specifics. We wanted to be sure, if possible, to cite concrete examples of any characteristic attributed to a periodical. The summaries were not intended to cover all the articles and features of a given periodical, but to refer only to those that seemed to be most typical of the periodical's editorial policy. In a few cases it was difficult to detect a definable editorial policy, but in most cases the policy was fairly evident.

The fourth step was to send drafts of the prepared content summaries to the editors of the respective publications, along with a request to have the drafts checked for accuracy and fairness. Nearly 90% of the editors had responded at the time of the final editing. Suggestions made by those who did respond were followed whenever possible, and some of their comments were added at the end of the final draft of the respective summaries.

Next arose the problem of arrangement. The summaries could, of course, have been arranged in a single alphabet, but the compiler felt that librarians might find it more useful to have the summaries arranged simply by broad categories. There was some reluctance to do so because of the possibility of being accused of labeling publications and the likelihood that some editors might not like their bedfellows. However, by creating a "Miscellaneous" category, some of these difficulties were overcome.

The end product is a list of titles arranged as follows:

```
Civil Rights and Negro ................... 14
Left of Center ........................... 42
Miscellaneous ............................ 21
Pacifist ................................. 12
Race Oriented ............................ 13
Right of Center .......................... 61
                                         ___
      Total ................... 163
```

This classification indicates the major areas of controversy in the U.S. today. Of greatest concern to the Right of Center is the danger of communism and "creeping socialism" and the preservation of order and "free enterprise." Some of the extremists on the Right believe in a conspiratorial theory of current affairs under which everything they dislike is attributed to a communist plot. Social welfare legislation is viewed as a threat. The Left of Center is primarily concerned with alleged injustices in the current social and economic system of the U.S. and with fundamental ways and means of bringing about greater fairness and equality. Those on the Left are not necessarily followers of radical socialist or revolutionist theories as is often assumed, but most believe in planning by government action, although they do not agree at all as to how to achieve improvements or what model to follow. Race-Oriented publications are primarily interested in the preservation of a pure, largely Anglo-Saxon race in the U.S. and view the Black race, and to a lesser extent, the Jewish people, as a threat to this objective. Civil rights and Negro groups strive primarily toward the betterment of the Negro in the U.S. Pacifists oppose warfare, which they view as the greatest threat to civilization, and lend their support to peace efforts. There is another area of controversy, that of sexual morality, that has not been covered in the present compilation; there seem to be very few regularly appearing publications exclusively devoted to promotion of a new outlook or opposed to traditional sexual modes. One might possibly place <u>Playboy</u> and <u>Cosmopolitan</u> in this category. Also not specifically covered in this compilation are religious beliefs, except atheism.

Those looking at this compilation critically should keep in mind that the compiler himself is painfully aware of some obvious deficiencies. The summaries would have been greatly improved if a larger number of issues could have been examined, if the history of each publication had always been dwelt upon, if the relationship of the publications to each other and to other publications had been covered, if a single person had been able to find time to read all the publications himself, if the periodicals could have been analyzed in greater depth, and if people had been available for the abstracting work who were more knowledgeable about all the subtle shadings of the various dissident and extremist groups.

In order to produce a list that would be reasonably current and useful, compromises had to be reached all along the way, and the end product is, therefore, far from perfect. This list should be regarded as a preliminary effort; it is expected that future editions will benefit from the lessons learned during the compilation of the initial attempt.

Please note that all circulation figures used were provided by the publications while the manuscript was being prepared. The editor can, therefore, not be responsible for their accuracy or for changes that have occurred since the original figures were received.

The list is expected to be useful, not only to librarians in selecting appropriate dissenting periodicals for display and use in their libraries, but also to students of social history. By reading these summaries, it should be possible to gain a fairly good insight into the political climate of the period, some of the issues that aroused controversy, the fears and aspirations animating many people who care a great deal about the future of the United States and of the world. Some of the spokesmen may be condemned as "crackpots" or "operators", but most of them appear to be sincere and dedicated believers. Generally they are dissatisfied with things as they find them and with the trend of events. They wish to make the United States a better country than it is.

A final note to fellow librarians: If one takes the "Library Bill of Rights" seriously, it would not seem inappropriate to try to subscribe to all the periodicals listed in this compilation and to display them regularly on open shelves in their library, possibly together as a special group in a separate section of the periodicals display area. The total annual cost of the subscription would probably not be much over $600.00. Readers in many communities and on many a campus will appreciate the opportunity to browse among these nonconformist publications. The display will attract attention and will serve an important educational function in alerting people to the existence of dissenting views in a society that has increasingly been tending toward consensus and conformity. If a library cannot afford to subscribe to or give shelf space to the entire list, the summaries of the content of the titles presented in this compilation should prove helpful as a guide to selection.

Also we ought to keep in mind that when we deal with such publications, the usual criteria of book selection, that is, substance and quality, do not apply. These fringe publications exist. We should not bar them from the public just because we may find them distasteful personally or uninteresting, or of low quality. They are important if they have an audience of subscribers or possibly for no other reason than that someone is willing to provide the money to subsidize them. Their audience may vary from less than a thousand to several thousands, and while many of the periodicals may have little appeal to the cultured and educated, we cannot afford to ignore them.

It is not sufficient for a librarian to wait until an interested party donates a subscription or until a specific title is asked for. It is an obligation to display as much of the spectrum of dissident opinion as space will allow, so that the library can serve as a sort of "Hyde Park Corner" where free communication, a clash of ideas, becomes a conspicuous new dimension of library service. Mary V. Gaver, President of the American Library Association, in her inaugural address in New York in July 1966, deplored the tendency of librarians not to view "their role as being one of actively seeking and participating in the world of conflict in which we live." Hopefully, this compilation may help to counteract some of this tendency.

Before concluding, I must pay tribute to my three successive collaborators, who toiled loyally and devotedly to bring this compilation into existence. First, there was Deborah Wood (now Mrs. Kilgore), a graduate of Earlham College, scholarly and exceedingly well-informed about political history, who organized the initial phases of the project and then moved on to become a librarian. Second, there was Mrs. Janet Ghent, a graduate of Oberlin College, who contributed her very considerable editorial and writing talents to the task of making the individual summaries more readable. Last, but by no means least, was Mrs. Lynn Reer, also an Oberlin graduate, who in a short period of time admirable succeeded in typing together the many pieces that had been left loose by the various people involved and brought the project to a reasonable state of completion. Without the dedication of these three young and extraordinarily bright co-workers and those whom they supervised, the project would not have seen the light of day. I am also grateful to Mrs. Lois Huisman, who added many final touches to the manuscript.

I must express my deep gratitude to the Jackson Social Welfare Fund Committee for providing seed money for this project. The project has proved to be of considerable direct benefit to the Labadie Collection, of the University of Michigan, in identifying many titles not previously collected and in gathering materials and data useful to its documentary preservation program. The knowledgeable Curator of the Labadie Collection, Mr. Edward C. Weber, was helpful in many ways, and some of the comments appearing at the end of the summaries were contributed by him.

Work on a supplement or new edition of the compilation may begin soon if funds can be obtained for this purpose. It is evident that births and deaths of periodicals in this area of dissident and minority expression are frequent and that a compilation requires regular updating to be of maximum usefulness to librarians.

                                        Robert H. Muller

Ann Arbor, Michigan
February, 1967

Chapter 1
CIVIL RIGHTS AND NEGRO

CORE-lator

Address: 200 W. 135th Street
    New York, New York 10030
Bimonthly; $2.00 per year
Circulation: 77,000

Publication Started: 1963
Format: 4-page Newsletter
Issues Examined: Jan.-Feb.;
    March-April; May-June, 1965

CORE-lator is published by the Congress of Racial Equality (CORE), an organization which works to eliminate racial discrimination by direct and non-violent methods. The newsletter is primarily concerned with disseminating news of CORE activities both in the North and the South. However, some articles deal with matters of general interest to people concerned with civil rights. The newsletter emphasizes the use of non-violent methods of direct action, including civil disobedience, in the struggle to break down the barriers of segregation and discrimination.

Editor's Response:
"The summary describing the CORE-lator is virtually correct. However, this newsletter has not been published for several months due to financial setbacks. We expect in the coming months to resume publication."

The Crisis

Address: The Crisis Publishing Co.,
    Inc.
    20 West 40th Street
    New York, New York 10018
Monthly (except June-July and Aug.-
    Sept. issues are combined); $1.50
    per year
Circulation: 130,000

Publication Started: 1910
Format: Small size, 48- to 64-
    page Magazine
Issues Examined: Several issues
    including October in 1965

The Crisis, the monthly magazine of the National Association for the Advancement of Colored People, concentrates on civil rights questions, but also includes articles on topics of more general interest. Regular features include editorials, letters from readers, book reviews, and reports from the various "battlefronts" of the civil rights activity--discrimination in unions and business, voting rights, and violence in the South. The magazine continually reports on progress made in the civil rights struggle.

Editor's Response:
Editor expressed no disapproval of statements made above.

Freedomways

Address: 799 Broadway
        New York, New York 10003
Quarterly; $3.50 per year
Circulation: 7,000

Publication Started: 1961
Format: Small size, 100- to 200-page Magazine
Issues Examined: Volume III, Nos. 1, 2, and 3 (1963) plus later issues

    Freedomways, "A Quarterly Review of the Negro Freedom Movement," covers significant Negro cultural and political activities relating to and supporting the "movement" for freedom and equality. Although Freedomways gives worldwide news coverage, it is mainly concerned with the freedom movements in the United States. The editor states that it is written with the goal of "a more vital kind of independent thinking that will be free of any specific political orientation."
    Freedomways discusses Negro artistic accomplishments: Ernest Kaiser writes comprehensive articles on Negro literature including "The Literature of the Negro Revolt," which deals with nonfiction about the freedom movements and with analytical discussions of the protest movements. Kaiser also contributes a feature on "Literature of Harlem" in the Summer, 1963 issue, "The Harlem Issue." Articles by Sylvester Leaks and Julian Mayfield on such figures as James Baldwin also appear in Freedomways, and each issue includes fiction and poetry.
    The magazine features an extensive book review section, focusing on books of interest to the Negro, including literature on Negro history, the protest and freedom movements, and Africa. Special issues which the editor states "are the only issues of this nature that have been published anywhere" include "The Africa Issue--Fall 1962," "The Harlem Issue--Summer 1963," "The Southern Freedom Issue--Winter 1964," "The Caribbean Issue--Summer 1964," "The Du Bois Memorial Issue--Winter 1965," and "The Mississippi Issue--Spring 1965."
    Among articles of cultural and historical interest, Freedomways includes "Civil War Centennial: Myth and Reality," an extensive survey assessing the contributions of the Civil War era to the struggle for Negro freedom. Another article, "The Negro in American Films," traces the history of Negro participation in the film industry from its inception to

the present.

Freedomways also presents articles directly concerned with the freedom movement and with economic, sociological, and political topics of interest to the Negro. "The White Southerner and the Integration Struggle" pleads for white recognition of Negro leadership. William Worthy, Calvin L. Hicks, and Benjamin Davis participate in a symposium entitled "Assault on Civil Rights." Davis compares the problems faced by the freedom movements--the restrictive legislation and the silencing of protestors--to the atmosphere of the police state present in the McCarthy era.

Editor's Response:
The editor expressed no disapproval. Comments have been incorporated in the text where appropriate.

Interracial Review

Address: Interracial Review
55 Liberty Street
New York, New York 10005
Monthly, except August; $4.00 per year
Circulation: 5,000

Publication Started: 1928
Format: 16- to 24-page Magazine
Issues Examined: February, June, and July, 1965

The Interracial Review, "A Journal of Christian Democracy," is published by the Catholic Interracial Council of New York. As its subtitle suggests, Interracial Review is concerned not only with questions of civil rights, but also with the larger question of social justice.

Some articles in the Interracial Review discuss Catholic ideas and activities. "When All of Us Will Forget," the interview of two Negro members of the Catholic Family Movement, deals with CFM's recent emphasis on race relations. Another article presents basic Catholic principles concerning the immorality of racial discrimination and applies them to questions asked by realtors concerning their moral obligations in the area of housing.

Other articles, such as two historical studies on labor union discrimination against the Negro, a discussion of the "subculture" of Negroes from the low socioeconomic classes, and an analysis of "What Next for the Civil Rights Movement?" by Nat Hentoff, present a variety of viewpoints, not necessarily connected with the Catholic Church.

Editorials on such topics as voting rights, poverty, and Catholic social action may be found in each issue.

Editor's Response:
"We would have it [the summary] as it is."

The Liberator

Address: Afro-American Research
Institute, Inc.
244 East 46th Street
New York, New York 10017
Monthly; $3.00 per year
Circulation: 15,000

Publication Started: 1961
Format: 20- to 30-page Magazine
Issues Examined: Jan., Feb., Mar., 1963; Apr., June, July, Aug., 1965

The Liberator regards itself as "the voice of the Afro-American protest movement in the United States and the liberation movement in Africa and America, which have developed along separate but parallel lines, with significant contact. The differences in conditions and tactics are less significant than the similarities and the existence of a common enemy."

The editor of The Liberator states that the magazine advocates "the concept of a multiracial, biracial, pluralistic society." He goes on to state that integration "leads the black people to nowhere." Len Holt says, "Make Harlem black, therefore beautiful": his article is critical of all Negro leadership in Harlem. Kattie Cumbo remarks, in "A Black Woman Looks at Integration," that the only "integration" she would like to see would be the integration of Negroes with Negroes, that is a greater cohesiveness of the Negro race in America and the establishment of economically self-sufficient Negro communities. Only the white man, she concludes, wants integration of the races.

Articles often advocate violence as the only effective weapon of the "Afro-American" against the "white power structure." An article entitled "Gen. Harriet Tubman, the Real Emancipator," a book review of Negroes with Guns, and an editorial express this "black power" view. Reports on the Harlem and Bedford-Stuyvesant riots appear to be favorable toward the rioters and bitterly critical of the nonviolent tactics of CORE, SNCC, and the NAACP. A cartoon characterizes Dr. Martin Luther King as throwing tranquilizers entitled "Bleed and Be Happy" to Harlem Negroes. Although one article by a civil rights worker in the South advocates nonviolence, the author agrees with other Liberator writers that integration should not be the goal of the civil rights movement.

Articles castigate the "white liberal," maintaining that the white man is the Negro's worst enemy, in America, Africa, and throughout the world. No matter what whites may say, the great majority of them believe in the inferiority of the Negro race, according to The Liberator. An article by Alvin Dark about the Negroes on the Giant baseball team and a speech by Senator Ellender support this view.

Articles on discrimination in the International Ladies' Garment Union and on narcotics addiction in Harlem emphasize the economic exploitation of the Negro by the "white capitalist." They equate the Negro with the proletariat and the white with the capitalist and combine traditional Marxist-leftist ideas with Negro nationalist views.

Many articles on African affairs are very favorably impressed with Africa's new leaders, her culture and society, and her economic and political viability.

The Movement

Address: 1316 Masonic Avenue
          San Francisco, California
Monthly; $1.00 per year
Circulation: 20,000

Publication Started: 1965
Format: 8-page tabloid Newspaper
Issues Examined: Oct., Nov., Dec., 1965

The Movement, published by the Student Non-violent Coordinating Committee of California, gives news of activities in which SNCC is involved and which SNCC supports, and discusses questions in which SNCC members and sympathizers would be interested. It attempts "to look critically at all activities that fall into the general category of 'grass-roots organizing,'" publishing "information that is not made available to people through the established press." The strike of agricultural workers in Delano, California, received considerable attention. News of the strike, how it was being conducted, and what was being accomplished, was presented, along with interviews of strike leaders and discussions of the questions at issue.

News of other actions, such as a boycott in Natchez, organizing among east coast migrant workers, voter registration, and school boycotts in Carroll County, Mississippi appears in The Movement.

Articles discussing such topics as "Mississippi Counterattacks the War on Poverty," House un-American Activities Committee strategy, San Francisco urban renewal programs, and "A Freedom Worker's View on War and Peace," may also be found in The Movement.

Editor's Response:
    "The summary seems to be fairly accurate and objective."

Muhammad Speaks

Address: Muhammad's Mosque No. 2
         634 East 79th Street
         Chicago, Illinois 60619
Biweekly; $5.20 per year
Circulation: Not ascertained

Publication Started: 1962
Format: 24- to 30- page tabloid Newspaper
Issues Examined: Volume IV, Nos. 8-10, 1965

    Muhammad Speaks, the journal of the "Black Muslins," often serves as a publication outlet for the leader of the Muslims, Elijah Muhammad. In such articles as "The True Solution" and "The Day of America's Downfall," Muhammad claims that the Bible and the Koran prove that whites are the Negroes' "created enemy," and that "Allah hates the wicked American whites and threatens to remove them from the face of the earth." Therefore, Negroes should not attempt to love their enemy (as the Christians admonish them to do); they should separate and leave the whites to Allah's punishment. Nonwhites all over the world should unite in Islam; integration is a false solution to racial problems and will never give the Negroes "freedom, equality, and justice," according to the Black Muslims.

    In Muhammad Speaks, one can find vigorous support for Elijah Muhammad as the one true "Messenger of Allah" and leader of the Negroes in America, especially since the defection of the late Malcolm X. Abdul Basit Nayeem, a Pakistani Muslim who is a regular contributor to Muhammad Speaks, writes much on this subject in the issues reviewed. The "lesson" from the "Holy Qu-ran," a regular feature, seems to deal with "hypocrites and those who have not realized that the Messenger was Allah, to whom obedience and deference are due." Muhammad himself presents an article on this subject in a January 1965 issue. The regular feature, "Women in Islam," also extols Elijah as the Messenger of Allah.

    Articles often appear in which people tell "how much Islam did for me." The Muslims do not permit the use of tobacco, alcohol, or narcotics, and they preach self-help and economic independence. Those who have found that their lives have improved since their conversion to Islam often express praise of these injunctions.

    Reports on affairs in Africa and Asia are written by Sylvester Leaks as well as by the syndicated columnist, Charles B. Howard. In one issue, Leaks writes about the revolt in Zanzibar and a Ghanaian discusses the Congo situation.

    A number of articles on current events in America are included in Muhammad Speaks. "Mississippi Women Spur Black Revolt" centers on the emergence of the Freedom Democratic Party. Another article reports on a symposium in which Negro psychiatrists present the view that racial prejudice is a sickness and that persons suffering from it should be forced to undergo treatment. Articles also cite the triumphs of Cassius Clay (Muhammad Ali).

A few human interest stories and a regular feature in the women's section, "Recipe of the Week," help to round out the newspaper. Often the back page of the issues presents a nutshell version of "The Muslim Program."

New South

Address: New South
    Southern Regional Council
    5 Forsyth Street, N.W.
    Atlanta 3, Georgia
Monthly when reviewed, to change
    to quarterly; $2.50 per year
Circulation: 2,200

Publication Started: 1946
Format: Small size, 16- to 20-page Magazine
Issues Examined: Feb., March, April, and June, 1965

New South, a publication of the Southern Regional Council, concentrates upon racial, social, and economic problems relating to the American South.

Articles emphasize the need for improving economic, political, and social conditions of the Negro. David Hunter, in "Macro and Micro Intervention against Poverty," points out that special attention should be given to the Negro as a group, since such a disproportionately high number of the poor are Negro. Margaret Long, editor, portrays the distressing situation of a very young Negro couple to illustrate the need for bettering Negro economic conditions. Pat Watters, in "Gregory and the Need for Grass," explains what a dozen college students (mostly white) did to clear a lot; the students hope to convert it into a playground for the children of an Atlanta Negro slum area.

Among the issues discussed is the problem of school desegregation: in a February editorial, Margaret Long shows how the Atlanta School Superintendent prevented integration in the Kirkwood School, an all-white school which was not being fully utilized at the time. The case of Dr. Guy H. Wells, reported by Dr. Wells and Eugene Patterson, relates the way in which the Board of Regents of Georgia State College for Women stripped Dr. Wells of his title of President Emeritus in 1956 because he had expressed sentiments in favor of "racial cooperation and school desegregation," and had become the secretary of the Georgia Council on Interracial Cooperation (forerunner of the Georgia Council of Human Relations). His title was reinstated in 1965.

Negro voter registration serves as another central topic in New South, which reprints a statement of protest and purpose read by 72 white

Alabamans who had joined the Selma-Montgomery march. The statement argues in favor of simplified registration forms and repeal of literacy test requirements. Another article illustrates the determination and accomplishments of voter registration workers as well as the lack of cooperation from city officials and the acts of violence and intimidation against the registration workers.

One article discusses the importance of the rural vote in relation to the impressive victory of Senator Goldwater in Mississippi. "The Battle of Books" states that the Negro has been excluded "not only from many aspects of the American present, but also from the American past," as history books and literature have "either ignored his presence or locked him to the meaningless roles that are vestiges of slavery."

Editor's Response:

"I found the descriptions of articles from New South factually accurate for the most part, if somewhat superficial, and certainly generous in length.

"In a spirit of inquiry, I'd like to raise a question regarding the classification of New South by your definition as 'dissident.' New South is not of the political right or left, because we are, here, studiously nonpolitical. And I wonder by what standard you would measure it to determine that it is 'nonconformist,' 'protest,' or 'minority opinion.' If you are making the classification by comparison with only the rest of the South, I fear you would have to include as 'dissident' virtually every mass circulation periodical in the country.

"In having supported for a number of years the same positions in regard to race as the most of civilized thought [sic] the United States Constitution, the consensus of the nation and now the will of the Congress of the United States, we resent being bracketed as we sometimes are in the South in the 'extremists on both sides' phrase with those who hold views based upon racism. And since the main concern of New South is race relations in the South, I raise the question of whether or not a similar kind of bracketing might not occur in your system of classification of the 'right' and 'left.' In other words, I don't think it would be either fair or accurate to classify our publication in the same category with most of the published materials of the right wing that I have seen--The Citizen, for example, of the Citizens Council organization.

"On this basis, we would request some statement of our disclaimer of fitting your definition of 'dissident' should you choose to include New South in your publication."

The Petal Paper

Address: East Publications Co.
         410 Pomelo Street
         Fairhope, Alabama 36532
Monthly; $3.00 per year
Circulation: 2,700

Publication Started: 1953
Format: 4-page tabloid size Newspaper
Issues Examined: May, June, and July, 1965

The Petal Paper is concerned mainly with the civil rights movement. The editor, P.D. East, is a famous gadfly journalist whose home state of Mississippi is "The Magnolia Jungle" of his book.

The paper particularly favors the work of Dr. Martin Luther King. "Dr. King and all such civil rights leaders are the exact opposite of Communists and just about the best bulwark we have in this country against Communists being able to take over the nation." In one article of the June issue discussing civil rights, the author says that the reason that progress has been made in this area is that "the Negro people, themselves, struggled to push it to the point where it could not be denied."

The paper contains articles reprinted from other publications. One from the Toledo Blade suggests that the Bill of Rights be rewritten to fit actual practices today and that it be renamed the Bill of Wrongs. Another from the Turlock, California Daily Journal praises the Brigham Young University for rejecting federal aid. The paper also contains many short news articles along with the editorials favoring civil rights. The June and July issues contain book reviews; humor is prevalent throughout the paper.

Editor's Response:
    "All OK."

SCLC Newsletter

Address: SCLC Newsletter
         334 Auburn Ave., N.E.
         Atlanta, Georgia 30303
Monthly (irregular): Contributions solicited
Circulation: Not ascertained

Publication Started: 1961
Format: 12-page Newsletter
Issues Examined: Oct.-Nov., 1965

The SCLC Newsletter is published by the Southern Christian Leadership Conference, a civil rights organization headed by the Rev. Martin Luther King. The newsletter's editor, Edward Clayton, writes editorials and occasional articles. Rev. King frequently writes for the newsletter as well. The newsletter reports on SCLC news, activities, and projects. It also includes reviews, advertisements of books, and reprints of cartoons.

The October-November, 1965 issue includes articles entitled "SCLC Puts Might of Its Organization Against 'Goldwaterism' to Aid in Win," "Of a Jail Mate and a Nobel Prize," "The 'Danger' of Intermarriage," "N.Y. Union Gives $6,000 to Civil Rights Groups," and "Nobel Prize Honors More than Mere Racial Changes."

Martin Luther King: The Peaceful Warrior and The Negro Politician, two new books written by Edward Clayton, receive favorable reviews in this issue.

The Southern Courier

Address: Room 1012
        The Frank Leu Building
        79 Commerce Street
        Montgomery, Alabama
Weekly; $5.00 per year in South;
    $10 per year in North; $25 patron
Circulation: 20,000

Publication Started: 1965
Format: 6-page Newspaper
Issues Examined: July 16; August 6, 20, and 28, 1965

The Southern Courier reports on developments in the South, mostly in Alabama, in the area of civil rights. The paper includes detailed reports on incidents that receive scant notice in the daily press. It also presents feature articles on some of the problems which desegregation, economic deprivation, and the political organization of the South entail. The Southern Courier also includes editorials and carries features on news of fairly general interest, and not always directly connected with civil rights. It features a considerable amount of photography. The newspaper represents no organization or group, but it takes a strong pro-civil rights stand.

Editor's Response:
    "Your summary of the Courier is accurate.
    "This newspaper represents objective journalism, considering the emotional nature of the subject matter; it is balanced and contains careful reporting. The editors are young journalism students. It could be called the New York Times of the civil rights papers."

The Southern Patriot

Address: 3210 W. Broadway
        Louisville, Kentucky 40211
Monthly; $3.00 per year
Circulation: 11,000

Publication Started: 1942
Format: 8-page tabloid Newspaper
Issues Examined: September, 1963;
   and October, 1965

The Southern Patriot is a monthly newspaper published by the Southern Conference Educational Fund (SCEF), a group which promotes civil rights activities in the South. The newspaper reports on events in the South related to civil rights, and concentrates on long-range perspectives and potentials rather than simply on items of current news value. It covers the plans of the civil rights movement in the South and political action in Washington likely to affect civil rights. Items of current interest, when reported, are related to the civil rights movement as a whole. This applies especially to the questions of peace, civil liberties, and poverty.

Editor's Response:
    "OK except for corrections." (Corrections have been incorporated into the text.)

The Voice

Address: Student Non-violent Coor-
    dinating Committee
    360 Nelson Street, S.W.
    Atlanta, Georgia 30313
Monthly to bimonthly; contributions
   of $3 or more to SNCC
Circulation: 40,000

Publication Started: 1959
Format: 4-page Newsletter
Issues Examined: August, September, 1965

The Voice is published sporadically by the Student Non-violent Coordinating Committee (SNCC), a civil rights group working in the South. The newsletter reports on the activities of SNCC and on incidents of racial "injustice" throughout the South. It reflects SNCC's interest in the development of indigenous leadership in the South. SNCC advocates direct nonviolent action, including civil disobedience, as a tactic in the struggle to break open the closed society of the South. The newsletter also contains articles which discuss problems of an intellectual nature concerning the civil rights movement, the role of whites in the movement, and ways of politicizing civil rights.

WCLC Newsletter

Address: 4802 McKinley
         Los Angeles, California
         90011
Monthly; Contributions solicited
Circulation: Not ascertained

Publication Started: 1965
Format: 16-page Newsletter
Issues Examined: June plus other issues in 1965

    The WCLC Newsletter is published by the Western Christian Leadership Conference, an affiliate of the Southern Christian Leadership Conference which is headed by Martin Luther King. The format and content of the WCLC Newsletter are similar to those of the SCLC Newsletter, published by the Southern Christian Leadership Conference.

    The WCLC Newsletter reports on the activities of both the SCLC and the WCLC. It gives coverage to the SCLC's campaign of "selective buying" and "economic withdrawal" directed against certain industrial and business interests in Alabama and also reports on Los Angeles WCLC activities, including gathering food, money, and clothing for people in Selma, Alabama.

    The WCLC Newsletter advertises and reviews literature published by the SCLC and the WCLC.

Chapter 2
LEFT OF CENTER

The Activist

Address: The Activist
    27-1/2 West College
    Oberlin, Ohio 44074
3 issues per year; $2.00 per year
Circulation: 2,000

Publication Started: 1961
Format: 40-page Magazine
Issues Examined: Spring, 1964; January, 1965

The Activist considers itself "an independent student review of political research and comment." A variety of subjects is covered in the magazine, from a generally leftist point of view. The Activist is edited and published by students; about one-third of the editorial comment is student-written.

Two articles in the Spring, 1964 issue of The Activist discuss the civil rights movement in terms of the larger issues and context of the more traditional Left. The articles, "Economics and the Civil Rights Crisis" and "only connect: reflections on the revolution," assess the civil rights movement in terms of its effect on the balances of political, social, and economic power in the USA. The authors of these articles believe that the civil rights movement will fail unless it correctly sees that the problems of unemployment, political alienation, city government, and income distribution are intimately connected with the problems of civil rights. However, these views are not stated simply as dogmatic generalizations.

At least one article in the issues reviewed, a critical analysis of the Lipset, Frazer, and Etzioni school of sociological analysis, was an academic effort as well as a vehicle for opinion. In this article the "sunshine school" was attacked for its acquiescense in "corporate capitalism" and in "organization." The view was expressed that the magical "pluralism" of a "healthy democracy" does not always solve society's problems or enable a "meaningful integration" of interests to be formed. The "professional critic" was chided.

Other articles include one written by an official of the Electrical Worker's Union, in which the author discussed the implications of automation for America. Raya Dunayevskaya, of News and Letters, contributed an article on the Sino-Soviet conflict; she indicted both Russia and China for failing to develop democratic, "humanist" Marxism and deplored the "State capitalism and arid theory" of both Communist giants.

Two other articles in the issues reviewed examine the current situation in Brazil and the Union of South Africa. The article on Brazil, written by a professor, analyzes the fall of Joao Boulart; it is severely critical of the Brazilian Left.

Book reviews and fiction round out the issues reviewed.

Editor's Response:
"Your synopsis is quite fair in its summary of what we are trying to do."

ADA Legislative Newsletter

Address: ADA Legislative Newsletter
    1223 Connecticut Avenue, N.W.
    Washington, D.C. 20036
Twice monthly while Congress is in session; $5.00 per year
Circulation: 2,000

Publication Started: 1960
Format: 4- to 6-page mimeographed Newsletter
Issues Examined: August 31, September 22, October 1, and October 13, 1965

The ADA Legislative Newsletter is published by the Americans for Democratic Action. Under the masthead is stated, "We summarize events in Congress as an information service to assist you in national affairs activities. We include brief analyses of legislative proposals together with factors of timing and politics as we see them." Most issues of the Newsletter are devoted to a single topic, and the Newsletter usually concentrates on issues relevant to liberal interests. For example, home rule for the District of Columbia, the politics of the anti-poverty program, the question of the governor's veto on anti-poverty projects, and the fight against the Dirksen Amendment, which would allow the states to take factors other than population into consideration in legislative apportionment, serve as subjects for discussion.

Also see the review of the other organ of this organization, ADA World, which follows immediately.

Editor's Response:
"Your summary for the guide is satisfactory."

ADA World

Address: ADA World
        1223 Connecticut Avenue, N. W.
        Washington, D.C. 20036
Monthly; Free to all ADA members, $5.00 per year to non-members
Circulation: 26,000

Publication Started: 1947
Format: 12-page tabloid Newspaper
Issues Examined: February, April, June, September, and October, 1965

The ADA World is published by the Americans for Democratic Action, an organization representing the liberal-left in American politics. The newspaper reports on ADA activities and presents ADA positions. One article reports that ten ADA leaders met with UN Ambassador Goldberg and called for a cessation of bombings in Vietnam and negotiation with the Viet Cong. Also, in the last year, the ADA took a very strong position in support of the "one man--one vote" decision of the Supreme Court requiring that state apportionment be based solely on population and presented defenses of this position in the ADA World. The ADA World discusses congressional activity in relation to liberal aims, particularly in articles such as "Strong Voting Rights Bill Enacted" and "Liberals Win First Battle to Preserve Court Decision." Also, the ADA World expresses support of the Freedom Democratic Party in its efforts to unseat the regular Mississippi representatives.

Editor's Response:
"We find no serious fault with the article you submitted."

American Dialog

Address: Room 804
        32 Union Square
        New York, New York 10003
Bimonthly (irregular); $4.50 per year
Circulation: 6,000

Publication Started: 1964
Format: 40-page Magazine
Issues Examined: Summer, 1966

American Dialog is a magazine of literary-social criticism and is sponsored by a group of leftist artists and intellectuals. In the issues examined, symposiums appear on the subjects of art and pornography, and on the poetry of Walt Whitman. Other regular features include poetry and artwork. The balance of the magazine consists of feature articles and fiction. Fictional work concentrates on the Negro freedom struggle and the criticism of conventional society; nonfiction articles more explicitly voice liberal political and social viewpoints. An interview with a female Member of the Indian Parliament who is also General Secretary of the National Federation of Indian Women and a Member of the Central Committee of the Indian Communist Party appears in one issue. Al Richmond, editor of the People's World, discusses the House Un-American Activities Committee's investigation of American artists and reviews Alvah Bessie's Inquistion in Eden. In one issue, the editors from American Dialog discuss with Gus Hall, leading Communist figure, the draft program of his party.

Other articles serve as vehicles for the formulation of impressions and opinions and include Lennox Raphael's "Carnival of the Poor," a description of the Mardi Gras in Brazil; Pete Seeger and Eslanda Robeson's "How can People Talk to Each Other?", and analytical reports from the World Writers' Congress in the German Democratic Republic.

Editor's Response:

"The draft could be improved if you would . . . indicate the wide array of writers and artists who appear in our pages and who sponsor the magazine. Our sponsors include: Linus Pauling, Louis Aragon, Bertrand Russell, Anton Refregier, Philip Evergood, Julian Beck, Shirley Graham DuBois, Alvah Bessie, and many others.

"Among those who have written for us are people of many variations from center leftward. We try to incorporate in our editorial material all people of good will, regardless of their politics--those who oppose war, racism and poverty. We have had, for example, Dorothy Day, Editor of the Catholic Worker, the Rev. Philip Berrigan, as well as people like Maxwell Geismar, Professor Asselineau of the Sorbonne, Prof. George Wickes of Harvey Mudd College . . . ."

American Socialist

Address: American Socialist
    American Socialist Organizing Committee
    1369 East 50th Street
    Chicago, Illinois 60615
Irregular; $3.00 per year
Circulation: 2,500 to 3,000

Publication Started: 1964
Format: 10- to 14-page tabloid Newspaper
Issues Examined: No. 3, No. 4, 1965

The American Socialist describes itself as the "Journal of the American Socialist Organizing Committee," which was formed in 1964 by chapters of the Young People's Socialist League expelled from the Socialist Party for ideological deviations to the left of the party's position. The journal "takes a militantly anti-liberal position." An anti-capitalist, anti-liberal, and anti-imperialist approach is quite evident in the <u>American Socialist</u>. Articles about the war in Vietnam claim that the war is an imperialist one whose "one and only purpose is to save a rotten branch of the capitalist system overseas." Articles on union activity emphasize militancy and admonish workers not to accept class collaboration on the part of their union leaders and to defy government intervention in labor activities. Unorganized strikes by institutional and governmental employees receive special coverage.

Attacks on liberal programs such as the "War on Poverty" appear in the <u>American Socialist</u>, which accuses these programs of failing to take fundamental action against poverty. The main accomplishment of these programs will be "to reveal all the defects of the capitalist system," according to the journal. The <u>American Socialist</u> employs material from and supports the position of the <u>Labour Worker</u>, an English publication, which it designates as "the leading left-socialist newspaper in England."

Antithesis

Address: P.O. Box 773
    San Francisco, California
Irregular (several issues per year)
Circulation: Not released by publication

Publication Started: August, 1964
Format: mimeographed Newsletter
Issues Examined: November-December, 1964; July, 1965

<u>Antithesis</u> expounds an orthodox Marxism-Leninism, vehemently disparaging pacifism and collaboration with capitalist activities as anti-socialist. The editors, who prefer to remain anonymous, present statements of policy in each issue which center about an attack on United States imperialism and monopolistic exploitation and a defense of proletarian attempts to seize power and move in revolutionary directions. Featured articles include essays on student movements in America, China, and Cuba, an editorial on the "Historical Struggle of the Vietnamese People for Independence," and a study on "The Economics of Imperialism."

Editor's Response:
"We believe that a fair and objective reading of <u>Antithesis</u>--whether one agrees with the political ideology expounded therein or not--would suggest that an attempt has been made at a reasoned analysis, with considerable documentation to support the arguments presented, of political events and issues of major contemporary importance.

"The following is a brief summary of each of the seven issues of

Antithesis that have been published:

"Issue I, August 1964: Editorial statement of 'where we stand' and a report on the founding convention of the W. E. B. DuBois Clubs of America criticizing their lack of a Marxist-Leninist outlook.

"Issue II, September 1964: 'The War in Vietnam': Contains a summary of the historical struggle of the Vietnamese people for independence and detailed account of events from the signing of the Geneva Agreements (1954) and the continual violations of these agreements by the United States to the incidents in the Gulf of Tonkin. And a statement of a Marxist-Leninist position on the war.

"Issue III, October 1964: Drawing on the writings of Lenin and the experience of Germany, _Antithesis_ presented its position on the coming Presidential election criticizing those radicals who argued for supporting Johnson against Goldwater. The analysis contained material from the political biographies of Johnson and Humphrey and considered the record of the Democratic party and placed the candidacy of Goldwater in the context of U.S. politics since 1945.

"Issue IV, November-December 1964: 'The Khrushchev Ouster and the Chinese Bomb': This issue contains an extensive analysis of the differing positions taken by the Chinese and Russian Communist Parties on the question of nuclear weapons and war.

"Issue V, January-March 1965: 'Student Movements': Contains a detailed factual and interpretive account of the Free Speech Movement at the Berkeley Campus of the University of California, and includes material on the nature of the modern University and the role of students in politics in the U.S.A. and in the Chinese and Cuban Revolutions.

"Issues VI and VII, July and November 1965: A Two-part study of 'U.S. Imperialism.' In the opinion of the editorial board, these two issues represent our most important, extensive and best efforts.

"Part One sets forth the thesis that the 'cold war' period has ended and that a period of 'hot war' has begun centering around the conflict of the expanded economic, military and political power of the U.S. Imperialism with the revolutions in the underdeveloped world. Vietnam and the Dominican Republic were taken as two major foci of this conflict. The role of the Chinese Communists as sources of inspiration and ideological leadership to the revolutionary movements around the world was pointed out.

"Part Two analyzes the economics underlying the political trends discussed in Part One, utilizing the Marxist theory of Imperialism. The politics of neo-colonialism, the role of 'wars of national liberation' and socialist planning are considered in this issue."

Bulletin of International Socialism

Address: Room 8
         243 East 10th Street
         New York, New York 10003
Biweekly; $2.00 per year
Circulation: 3,000

Publication Started: 1964
Format: 4-page mimeographed Newsletter
Issues Examined: December 13 and 27, 1965

    The Bulletin of International Socialism is published by the American Committee for the Fourth International, a small Trotskyist group in the United States. This group states that it is in political solidarity with the International Committee of the Fourth International. This international Trotskyist tendency includes the Socialist Labour League in Great Britain, the Organization Communiste Internationale in France, and the League of Hungarian Revolutionary Socialists.
    The Bulletin covers a variety of national and international events of interest to radicals from a Marxist point of view. For instance, developments in the trade union movement and in the Negro movement are covered. The paper strongly advocates the building of a labor party in the United States as the next big step for American workers.
    The Bulletin contains a good deal of polemical material on other radical organizations such as the Socialist Workers Party, Progressive Labor, Students for a Democratic Society, the Spartacist League, etc. These groups are accused of being "revisionist," having "abandoned the class struggle."
    It also analyzes international developments such as the Vietnam War, developments within the Soviet Bloc countries, Cuba, Indonesia, England, and Western Europe. Some of this material is written in this country and some is submitted by co-thinkers in other countries.

Editor's Response:
    The above version was revised and rewritten by the Bulletin's editor; it is therefore more comprehensive than the copy we submitted to him and brings us up to date. In his letter, the editor mentioned that the Bulletin is one of the few Socialist publications which comments extensively on other Socialist tendencies.

The Catholic Worker

Address: 175 Chrystie Street
   New York, New York 10002
Monthly (except July-August combined); 25¢ a year
Circulation: 85,000

Publication Started: 1933
Format: 8-page tabloid Newspaper
Issues Examined: March, April, May, June, 1965

The Catholic Worker describes itself as "the organ of the Catholic Worker Movement." The issues reviewed present the goals and beliefs of this movement.

An article on "Catholic Worker Positions" maintains that the present social order "generally called capitalist" is not just: production is for profit, not need, the individual is subjected to the demands of the profit motive, and human values are disregarded. Finally, the oppression of the lower classes results in hatred and conflict, both of which are morally wrong, according to the article. Therefore, the present social order should be changed by nonviolent direct action, and a decentralized communal social order should be established. Other articles commemorate Peter Maurin, the founder of the Catholic Worker Movement, giving insight into the aims and beliefs of the movement. Maurin, an educated man of southern-French-peasant descent, and Dorothy Day, a Catholic convert from Communism, set up a program in the 1930's which included establishing "Houses of Hospitality" to aid the poor and printing The Catholic Worker newspaper. They also set up communal farms. Maurin expressed the view that the object of all social institutions should be the development of all aspects of the individual; he termed this view "personalism."

The Catholic Worker includes articles on civil rights. "A Hard Row to Hoe" by Henry Anderson relates the Catholic Worker Movement's conception of rural organization to the needs of the Southern Negro and the Southern agricultural economy. Other articles give witnesses' reports on recent civil rights activities: Nicole D'Entremont describes her visit to Selma before and during the march, and Tom Connell gives a participator's views of "The Berlin Wall in Selma, Alabama." Priest Philip Berrigan discusses "The Black Man's Burden" and the debt which America owes to the Negro.

Peace and nonviolence also receive central attention. In one issue, Lewis Mumford presents an "Open Letter" to President Johnson about the war in Vietnam, and the journal reprints a speech by Priest Daniel Berrigan given before a rally held to protest the war. A "Petition of American Citizens to Pope Paul VI for Further Leadership in the Work for World Peace" also appears.

Issues also cover the activities of Catholic Worker Movement personnel and organizations and include extensive correspondence.

Editor's Response:
Minor changes, now incorporated in the text, were suggested. Approval or disapproval was not indicated.

Challenge - Desafio

Address: GPO Box 808
    Brooklyn 1, New York
Monthly (started as a weekly, changed to monthly in 1966)
Circulation: Not Ascertained

Publication Started: 1964
Format: Originally a 10-page Newspaper, now a 24-page Magazine
Issues Examined: V. I, Nos. 1, 3, 6, 12; June 11 and 27, July 18, September 12, 1964

Challenge, New York organ of the Progressive Labor Party, gears its articles almost exclusively to the Negro and Puerto Rican communities in New York City, printing several of its pages in Spanish. Major subjects discussed include discrimination, police brutality, and slum housing conditions. One of the issues reviewed displays a huge red headline, "Police War on Harlem," with a full page photo of a man who had allegedly been partially blinded by a Harlem policeman. Issues contain reports on specific cases of police brutality.

Efforts of individuals and groups to fight the "slumlords" receive extensive coverage. One issue exposes a so-called "eviction racket" in this connection, and articles support the rent strikes. Reports on slum conditions do not limit themselves exclusively to the problems of Puerto Rican and Negro slums. The front page of a 1964 issue of Challenge shows a 63-year-old white man standing on the sidewalk beside his furniture after having been evicted from an apartment in which he and his wife were said to have lived for thirty-five years. Challenge emphasizes the view that New York City is doing nothing to improve slum conditions and that the city owns some of the worst buildings and refuses to rehabilitate them.

Each issue features a column entitled "without exploitation," which compares socialism to capitalism and tries to explain socialism's "many advantages" in simple language.

Editor's Response:
"The magazine "no longer carries the title 'without exploitation,' and the main emphasis has shifted from the police brutality to reflecting life in the ghettos in general, on the campuses, and in the shop. It also carries much anti-war and anti-imperialist and pro-communist material."

Despite Everything

Address: 1937-1/2 Russell Street
        Berkeley, California 94703
Quarterly; $2.00 per year
Circulation: usually under 1,000

Publication Started: 1964
Format: 16- to 40-page mimeographed Magazine
Issues Examined: March, July 1965; and January, 1966

    Despite Everything is a publication whose purpose is "to be of the service that it can to be Movement (this has meant the Civil Rights Movement. Now, the meaning insensibly broadens, as it should). That means: provide predictions that turn out, true information not available elsewhere, analyses that are of demonstrable value, proposals for action that are useful, and always to tell the truth, on the theory that people are entitled to it."

    This magazine represents a strong left view. It is not concerned so much with theory as it is with specific issues and practical action. It is very much opposed to President Johnson, attributing to him "pious dissembling and the usual schizophrenia." It attacks Martin Luther King as "an agent of Johnson and the establishment in the Movement"; and James Baldwin for not "show[ing] up at the right time and place," and for being a businessman after all. The writers of this magazine also are very skeptical of the war on poverty.

    Despite Everything reports on such activities as a nursery school for Negroes in Albany; it supports the California grape pickers' strike, the rights of people on welfare, and free universities. It is concerned with Vietnam (where "colored people are being slaughtered in a war not of their making"), and Rhodesia (Wilson is seen as a "best friend of Smith").

    With regard to Despite Everything's position on communism, the editor charges with backwardness, those "who believe that Mao's China is progressive." Despite Everything leans toward working out its own practical position rather than endorsing communism, although it certainly opposes capitalism, as the article on how capitalism led to the war in Vietnam shows.

    The following will help define more closely the "Movement" that this magazine speaks for: "The line of division between those who are of the Movement and those who aren't does not fall where you would imagine, between those 'close,' friendly, and sympathetic, and the others. It falls between those taken up to a greater or lesser extent in the Commodity system that surrounds and invades every positive thing in this society and the other. It's that system . . . that in the end runs against the grain of the Movement for itself."

    Another editorial comment is as follows: "In this year's American electoral politics, DE finds little positive in the Liberal Democrat campaigns, nor in those of Julian Bond in Georgia and Robert Scheer in California. It favors only the independent third-party movement promoted by the Student Non-violent Coordinating Committee in Alabama and other states of the deep south."

Editor's Response:
" . . . the résumé is adequate and even--it seems to me--indicates quite a bit of perceptivity on the part of the student who did it, not to say sympathy."

Dissent

Address: 509 Fifth Avenue
         New York 17, New York
Bimonthly; $5.00 per year
Circulation: 7,500

Publication Started: 1954
Format: Small size, 40- to 100- page Magazine
Issues Examined: Spring, 1964; Winter, 1965

"A Quarterly of Socialist Opinion," Dissent is somewhat similar in both form and content to New Politics; both contain articles of some of the same authors, although Dissent seems to be less committed to Marxism.

Each issue contains articles, short comments, book reviews, and one special report. The subject matter covers analyses of current events and problems, historical presentations, and discussions primarily of intellectual interest in the fields of political and ethical philosophy, economics, and political science. Throughout, the journal emphasizes the relevance of principles of democratic, undogmatic socialism to the topics discussed.

A special report on the New York City school crisis in 1964/65 analyzes grass roots opinion about integration and bussing as well as the larger problem of school-system politics in New York City. Another article, "South Bend: Tragedy at Studebaker," examines in detail the problems caused by the mass layoffs which occurred when Studebaker closed its auto production plant in South Bend. "The Agony of Italian Socialism" surveys the Italian political scene and the problems faced by the Socialist Party in that context. Also in the field of current affairs, "The Negro Movement: Beyond Demonstrations" discusses the relationship of Negro protest movements to the larger aims of the socialist Left.

Among historical presentations in Dissent, a study of the policies of Sidney Webb while he was Colonial Secretary in the first Labour Government of Great Britain relates Webb's policies to specific attitudes characteristic of Fabianism. Another study documents censorship of the writings of Maxim Gorki and other Russian authors on Jewish matters.

Theoretical issues and questions of intellectual interest form a significant part of the subject matter in Dissent. One author discusses philosophy in the Soviet Union, stressing the inevitability of diversity in modern philosophy, even in the Soviet Union, where diversity is not openly acknowledged. Raymond Williams and Marshall Berman attempt to explain the relationship between the diverse political philosophies of the English Romantics and the presumably common Romantic philosophical and esthetic presuppositions which underlie their thought. Also in the field of intellectual history, Lewis Coser's article, "China, Russia, and the Intellectuals," examines the relationship between the more philosophical views of the French *philosophes* and their adulation of Russian and Chinese despotism. A scholarly study entitled "The Prospects for Pluralistic Communism" reviews the characteristics of several Communist countries in the world of today.

Facts (American-Soviet Facts)

Address: Facts
National Council of Soviet-American Friendship
156 Fifth Avenue
Suite 304
New York, New York 10010
Bimonthly; Contributions solicited
Circulation: 14,000

Publication Started: 1964
Format: Small size, 20- to 28-page Magazine
Issues Examined: October, December, 1964; February, April, June, 1965

Facts, which consists of reprints from the New World Review, is published by the National Council of American-Soviet Friendship to provide "nationwide circulation to thousands of individuals--presently some 14,000; to the farm, trade union, religious and Negro press, to journals of public opinion and to cultural and educational institutions including 3,700 public, college and university libraries." The magazine consists of news items about the Soviet Union grouped under regularly-featured categories: "Cultural and Scientific Exchange" includes an article on the "Collected Edition of Sinclair Lewis" and a report of a Georgian scientist lecturing in America; "Progress and Problems in the USSR" includes articles on reductions in medicine prices and on the restoration of privately-owned livestock rights; "International Trade" covers news of the expansion of the Soviet Merchant Fleet and an article entitled "Professors for Easing Trade Curbs." Concerning American-Soviet Relations," there are articles on "Russia, the US and Vietnam" and US and USSR See Gains in Settling UN Dispute."

Free Student

Address: 2300 Broadway
    New York, New York 10024
Seems to be bimonthly; $5.00 per
    year or $2.50 to students
Circulation: 10,000

Publication Started: 1965
Format: 8- to 20-page tabloid
Issues Examined: Nos. 2, 3, 6,
    and 7
Mail returned, Jan., 1967

The Free Student is published by the May 2nd Movement, formed in May, 1964, "to fight against a politics of default, specifically by organizing student protest and revolt against our government's savage war on the people of Vietnam. The May 2nd Movement, the youth group of the Progressive Labor Party, supports the activities and aims of the South Vietnamese National Liberation Front (Vietcong). The Free Student gives news of the situation in Vietnam and the activities of those opposed to U.S. Vietnam policies. The journal attacks "U.S. imperialism" and upholds a Marxist position, on the subject of imperialism, especially in articles on the Dominican Republic and Malaysia. News of student activism also appears in the Free Student, along with stories on the new "free universities" and articles which attack the established institutions. The journal also presents "International Student News," in which leftist student activism serves as the primary topic.

Editor's Response:
    "It is mostly correct excepting . . . the fact that the May 2nd. Movement has dissolved."
    The following is from the dissolution statement of the May 2nd Movement:
    "We had two choices: 1) To continue to build M-2-M. 2) To dissolve M-2-M and work as members and activists to build the existing mass organizations that are changing and becoming radicalized through struggle . . . . We choose to work in and build the existing radical organizations --our goal is the development of a mass socialist student movement in America. To accomplish these ends:
    1. We dissolve the May 2nd Movement
    2. The Free Student newspaper will continue to publish. It will try to a) Serve as a center of active debate, of radical views and analysis, Marxist and non-Marxist, on the key ideological and programmatic questions before the movement. b) Encourage and participate in a full scale student assault against the establishment universities which, as the ideological prep school for U.S. imperialism, have refined the techniques of mis-education, rote learning, compartmentalization, and total control over students' lives, in an effort to turn out faithful and fully alienated servants of monopoly capital. The newspaper will continue to have an

anti-imperialist editorial line. The present editorial board will continue until they are joined or replaced by others of the movement . . . . "

Frontier

Address: 1434 Westwood Boulevard
    Los Angeles, California
    90024
Monthly; $4.00 per year
Circulation: 6,000

Publication Started: November, 1949
Format: 28-page Magazine
Issues Examined: July, September, and November, 1965

    Frontier is a moderately liberal publication dealing with problems of national significance. It opposes (a) the far right as being childish in its tactics, (b) the war in Vietnam as being a "war of aggression," and (c) the House Committee on Un-American Activities because it "began as a front for every squalid, reactionary element in the country and has remained faithful to its trust." It favors the civil rights movement which it believes has "aroused the American moral conscience," and the campus demonstrations which it praises as "just about the best thing that has happened to American education."

    The July issue contains an article entitled "Privacy: Our Vanishing Freedom." In this article it is stated that the U.S. has been using "police state tactics," and as an example, Frontier cites the fact that the Post Office Department turns over mail of delinquent taxpayers to the Internal Revenue Service. To sum up Frontier's attack on these "tactics," it states: "Spying in any form smacks of 'gestapo' methods, and is incompatible with every principle of human decency for which our nation stands."

    The September issue deals with the Los Angeles riots in the Watts area. It refers to the area as a "Negro ghetto." In the articles involving the riots, Frontier states its belief that there was no Communist inspiration for what happened. The publication calls for greater understanding of the Negro problem.

    The magazine is set up much like Time magazine. There is a section of editorials on current news, and sections for book reviews, theater, art, music and films. Also throughout are cartoons reflecting Frontier's unfavorable attitude toward the Vietnam Policy of the Johnson Administration as well as other problems, and cartoons connected with specific articles.

    Frontier believes that President Johnson has done more toward solving the Negro problem than any other president, and the magazine is in general accord with the domestic program of the President.

Editor's Response:
Editor expressed no disapproval.

Hammer and Steel Newsletter

Address: Box 101
         Mattapan Station
         Boston, Massachusetts
Monthly; $1.50 per year
Circulation: Not ascertained

Publication Started: 1961
Format: 6- to 8-page mimeographed Newsletter
Issues Examined: July, September, and November, 1965; January and March, 1966

Hammer and Steel Newsletter is a publication representing one of the "Marxist-Leninist versions of Communism in the United States and attacking the United States Communist Party for its revisionism. Its goal is the establishment of a Marxist-Leninist Party in the United States." It also speaks out repeatedly against pacifism and imperialism. It holds the Chinese Communist Party up as an example of a good Marxist-Leninist Party. To illustrate how extreme in its position the Hammer and Steel Newsletter is, it should be noted that it vehemently attacks Norman Thomas for "vicious rotten Chauvanism," Herbert Aptheker for having "a rotten purpose" for his Vietnam trip, and Gus Hall for having a "clique."

This publication is theoretical in emphasis. It takes various topics such as the "Afro-American" question, the 81 Party Statement, the war in Vietnam, or the publication of a policy article by Chinese Defense Minister Lin Pao, and analyzes them in light of its own views. For example, it attacks the 81 Party Statement for endorsing the revisionist Communist Party in the United States, and thus supporting "an unprincipled compromise." It analyzes the Negro situation in the U.S. as being not a matter of racial discrimination, but rather national oppression. It says that the Negroes should establish an Afro-American nation of their own in the "Black Belt" region of the South.

Editor's Response:
"Acceptable for the kind of guide you are compiling if certain alterations are made: (1) Our criticism of the 81 Party Statement of 1960 as presented in your summary is very incomplete. The more important criticism that we made of this document is that it did not prepare the peoples of the world for the type of struggle that has taken place since 1960. Great armed struggles have taken place in Vietnam, Algeria, Cuba, the Dominican Republic, the Congo and Watts while the 81 Part Statement led the people to believe that peaceful coexistence and peaceful transition would follow. (2) There is another aspect of our work which distinguishes us from other so-called anti-imperialist organizations in the U.S.

We do not sign our material. We do not have illusions that anti-imperialists will receive preferential treatment from U.S. imperialism just because they live within her national boundaries. We believe that it is inconsistent for any group which proclaims U.S. imperialism to be the main enemy of the world's people to carelessly expose its members to imperialism's reactionary forces."

I. F. Stone's Weekly

Address: 5618 Nebraska Ave., N.W.
       Washington, D.C.
Weekly; $5.00 per year
Circulation: 30,000

Publication Started: 1952
Format: 4-page Newsletter
Issues Examined: January 25, February 1, 8, 15, 22, March 1, and May 31, 1965

I. F. Stone's Weekly, an independent newsletter, which Stone himself calls radical, concentrates primarily on coverage of foreign affairs and international relations, although domestic affairs also receive coverage.

Many recent issues are devoted to criticizing the war effort in Vietnam. Stone's comments on this subject fall into two broad categories: 1) He attempts to expose the mistakes which have characterized the Administration's policies in Southeast Asia; 2) He maintains that the U.S. Government's concept of the war, as presented in its White Paper on Vietnam, is erroneous, as the Vietcong is not dependent upon North Vietnam, although it has received some aid from the North.

Stone also inveighs against U.S. Government control of news from South Vietnam, arguing that certain stories either never get printed or are modified substantially. Stone also deplores U.S. intervention in the Congo to aid the Belgians, not because the U.S. Government did not have the right to intervene, but because it should have realized that other African states could construe any type of intervention as "aggressive neocolonialism."

In the area of domestic affairs, Stone calls for stronger civil rights legislation, the abolition of HUAC, and the strengthening of civil liberties.

In the May 31, 1965 issue, which I. F. Stone characterizes as "a good sample . . . illustrating the independent point of view," the major article compares the U.S. intervention in the Dominican Republic to the Russian intervention in Hungary. These interventions resulted essentially from the desires of the United States and the Soviet Union to preserve spheres of influence over strategic territories by imposing governments upon them. Reporting on Senate hearings concerning a "planning for peace" resolution which would require more concrete work on disarmament programs to be undertaken, Stone reveals the extent to which the U.S. Arms Control and Disarmament Agency works hand in hand with the Pentagon.

In this issue, Stone expresses pleasure at the May 1965 Supreme Court decision to prohibit the screening of foreign mail coming into the country. He also notes that the American Baptist Convention called for talks with Red China and negotiations with "all groups" in Vietnam.

Industrial Worker

Address: 2422 North Halstead Street
   Chicago, Illinois 60614
Monthly; $3.00 for 52 issues
Circulation: Not ascertained

Publication Started: 1916
Format: 4-page Newspaper
Issues Examined: July, August, 1965

The Industrial Worker is the "official organ of the Industrial Workers of the World" (IWW), which stands for an anarcho-syndicalist approach to union organization. An apolitical organization founded in 1905, the IWW distrusts government in general and considers wars to be the business of governments which a working-class solidarity should oppose. The publication expresses these views and also presents news of conditions among agricultural workers and of the prospects for union organization in this area. The IWW is active in some west coast agricultural and fruit growing regions.

Other labor news, such as news of the Philadelphia teamsters strikes, and book reviews are also published.

Insurgent

Address: 954 McAllister Street
   San Francisco, California
   94115
6 times a year; $1.25 per year, single copy 25¢
Circulation: 5,000

Publication Started: 1965
Format: 32-page Magazine
Issues Examined: May-June, 1965; July-August, 1965; March-April, 1966

Insurgent is the national periodical of the W. E. B. DuBois Clubs of America. It attempts "to give the magazine a content that will interest young people who are not yet active in any radical movement." It is basically concerned with the civil rights movement, but defends the right for all kinds of demonstrations. The magazine describes the Berkeley demonstrations as, "the most inspiring movement in this nation's history." Strong opposition to the war in Vietnam is voiced with Insurgent's urging, "We must press for an end to our government's brutal war there." Concerning the question as to whether the organization is subversive or a

Communist front, the editors answer: "We in the DuBois Clubs do not deny that there are Communists in our organization, and we defend the right of Communists to participate in the political life of our country." Concerning the legality of the current tactics of the civil rights demonstrations, _Insurgent_ states its position with the question, "When the whole structure of government and force of economic power is bent on denying people (black and white) their rights, how can anyone insist that the drive for redress of grievances be contained within the framework of law and order and established political institutions?"

Each of the issues examined contains editorials and essays on a wide range of topics from James Dean and Cassius Clay, to a "discussion of fashions, manners, and mores in our time," to the political subjects of civil rights and the war in Vietnam. Also included are poetry, book reviews, and cartoons.

Editor's Response:
"The summary of _Insurgent_ you sent me is quite acceptable."

International Socialist Review

Address: 116 University Place
        New York, New York 10003
Bimonthly; $2.50 per year
Circulation: 3,000

Publication Started: 1934 (then entitled _Fourth International_, name changed in 1956)
Format: 32- to 40-page Magazine
Issues Examined: Spring, Summer, Fall, 1964; Winter, 1965

The _International Socialist Review_ is the theoretical organ of the Socialist Workers' Party (Trotskyist); it presents discussions of Marxism-Leninism and Trotskyism. The review also covers news within the Fourth International and discusses the prospects around the world for revolutionary socialism. The writing in the ISR is characterized by an emphasis on theory, analytic technique, and polemics.

William F. Warde writes on philosophical questions: he covers a debate held in Paris between existentialist and Marxist thinkers on the subject, "Is Nature Dialectical?" In this article, he discusses present-day theories of dialectical materialism in relation to the natural sciences. Warde also contributes an article on "The Importance of the Individual in History," attempting to reconcile Trotsky's views with traditional, more rigid concepts of historico-economic determinism. In this article, he engages in polemics against a former Marxist, Sidney Hook, and an avowed Marxist, Isaac Deutscher. The ISR displays an interest in Deutscher's biography of Trotsky, although critical of its merits.

In the issues reviewed, two matters of interest to members of the newly-reconstitueted Fourth International receive considerable coverage: the situation in Ceylon and the alleged "left-sectarianism" (left of Socialist Workers' Party and the Fourth International) of the British Socialist Labour League. Trotskyist parties consider themselves revolutionary parties; that is, they do not allow any political collaboration with the capitalist "class enemy." However, they do abide by Lenin's theory of "democratic centralism," requiring a strong party-political organization and advocating a united class-struggle and the establishment of a dictatorship of the proletariat. Thus, they continually strive to avoid a social-democrat stance (which they regard as "rightist") and anarcho-syndicalism (which they regard as "leftist"); they also oppose Stalinist totalitarianism and "state capitalism." Such cases as the Ceylonese sections of the Fourth International joining a "bourgeois" coalition government and the ultra-leftism of a British group call for great ingenuity in presenting a "correct" Trotskyist interpretation.

The magazine also reviews the state of world revolutionary forces, presenting analyses of the Chilean political scene (before the election of Frei) and discussing the activities and opportunities of the Left front. Articles staunchly defend the Cuban Revolution as instrumental in bringing about a continuous advance toward genuine socialism in Cuba.

Affairs pertaining solely to the United States receive limited coverage. The journal analyzes the document published by the "Ad Hoc Committee for the Triple Revolution" from a Trotskyist point of view.

Editor's Response:

"In the article your summary mentions, William F. Warde treats the question of the relative importance of the objective and subjective factors in determining the emergence of Stalin. On this point, the disagreement with Deutscher is one of judgment on a particular question and not one of analytical method."

Liberation

Address: 5 Beekman Street
          New York 38, New York
Monthly; $5.00 per year
Circulation: 10,000

Publication Started: 1956
Format: 32- to 48-page Magazine
Issues Examined: January, February, and March, 1965

Liberation, a periodical of radical opinion, concentrates primarily on questions of nonviolent action and pacifism. However, it also concerns itself with the more traditional subject matter of the left, the inter-relationship of economic, social, and political problems. Although several of the regular contributors to Liberation consider themselves democratic socialists, this characterization could not apply to all of the contributors.

Articles discussing peace and nonviolence include "Unilateralism Reconsidered," by A. J. Muste, who maintains that peace organizations must not modify their strong stands on disarmament (which include sanction of the concept of unilateralism) in the hope that governments will listen to them. These organizations must take a stand of opposition to the governments of nation-states and the militarism characteristic of them. Liberation opposes the war in Vietnam and prints a "Declaration of Conscience" against the war formulated by the Catholic Worker, the Committee for Nonviolent Action, the Student Peace Union, and the War Resister's League in its March 1965 issue. In the area of nonviolent action, the Winter issue of 1964/65 contains one of a series of "prison notes" written by Barbara Deming, of the "Biracial Quebec-Washington-Guantanamo Peace Walk," during which she and other members of this group were imprisoned in Albany, Georgia. Liberation also reprinted the text of Martin Luther King's speech upon being presented the Nobel Peace Prize.

The issues present extensive criticism of the Warren Commission Report; Vincent J. Salandria, a Philadelphia lawyer, maintains that evidence was falsified in order to enable the Commission to stand by the theory that only Oswald was involved in the assassination attempt.

It was in Liberation that the "Ad Hoc Committee for the Triple Revolution" first published its statement on "Jobs, Income and Cybernation." Gerald Piel and Robert Theobald (signers of the statement) continue to write on the subject of automation and its social and economic effects in the pages of this periodical.

Past issues of Liberation also present material on Cuba, with a pro-Castro slant, written by Dave Dellinger.

Paul Goodman notes in his preface to Seeds of Liberation, a book of selected essays taken from the pages of Liberation, that the magazine has been characterized from its inception as the organ of a group of existentially "engaged" critics of society and believers in nonviolence. It means to oppose the "Liberal Establishment" but its voice is not that of the traditional Socialist-Communist left.

The Militant

Address: 873 Broadway
    New York, New York 10003
Weekly; $3.00 per year
Circulation: 9,000

Publication Started: 1928; became New Militant, 1934; Socialist Appeal, 1937; Militant, 1941
Format: 8-page tabloid Newspaper
Issues Examined: September 13, 20, 27, 1965, plus some earlier issues

The Militant, "published in the interests of the working people," is a weekly paper reflecting the views of the Socialist Workers' Party (Trotskyist). The journal covers labor, the Negro protest and civil rights movements, and other domestic news, as well as foreign affairs. The Militant also reports on legal cases involving freedom of the press and freedom of speech.

In the area of domestic and labor news, the Longshoremen's strike is particularly singled out as an example of militancy among rank and file workers. An analysis of the Abel-McDonald struggle for the presidency of the Steelworkers Union presents the view that Abel has responded to rank and file dissatisfaction and would be more militant than McDonald if he were elected. The Militant also discusses police brutality in New York City and other metropolitan areas and presents a report on the Berkeley free speech movement.

Extensive analysis of foreign affairs includes coverage of the Vietnam situation. One article maintains that United States "advisors needed bodyguards to protect them from the South Vietnamese troops." A statement by Senator Morse on Vietnam is printed in full. The Congo and Cuba are also discussed.

Much space is devoted to various factions of the Negro movement, with focus on separatists and integrationists as well as independent Negro political activities in Mississippi. The Socialist Workers' Party also takes particular interest in the late Malcolm X.

Articles about the sedition trials of the Young Socialists at Indiana University also appear, with reports about a professor who lost his job because of alleged Communist sympathies.

The Trotskyist orientation of the newspaper can be detected in its attacks on Soviet bureaucracy, its staunch advocacy of revolution, its opposition to the Stalin-Khrushchev versions of peaceful coexistence with the capitalist camp, and its warnings against class collaboration. However, The Militant attempts to appeal primarily to the masses, rather than to present the opinions of a socialist sect.

Editor's Response:
"I think the brief description of our paper by your assistant is on the whole fair and adequate.

"The SWP is sometimes referred to as 'Trotskyist'* although that is

---

*A "Trotskyist" is, historically, one who followed Leon Trotsky in his break with Stalin and his subsequent setting up of the Fourth International in 1938 as a rival to the Third International controlled by Stalin and the Communist Party of the U.S.S.R. Theoretically, Trotskyists condemn "Stalinist bureaucracy" and advocate "permanent revolution" as opposed to "peaceful coexistence."

not its own self-designation.

"Since you refer to [the late] Malcolm X, you might be interested in adding the fact that early in 1965 he stated publicly that The Militant is one of the best papers anywhere."

Monthly Review

Address: 116 West 14th Street
        New York, New York 10011
Monthly (11 issues per year); $6.00 per year
Circulation: 8,500

Publication Started: 1949
Format: Small size, 48- to 64-page Magazine
Issues Examined: December, 1964; February, March, April, 1965

The Monthly Review describes itself as "an independent socialist magazine." Its "independence," however, does not imply that the journal has abandoned Marxism-Leninism. The Monthly Review takes a revolutionary stance.

Two regular features, "Review of the Month" and "World Events" present analyses and commentary on current events and discussions of economic questions, for example, "The Kennedy-Johnson Boom," "The U.S. in Vietnam: The Road to Ruin," and the fall of Khrushchev. These reviews are written by the editors. In "The Kennedy-Johnson Boom," the editors express the belief that the period of economic expansion created by the tax cut does not substantially mitigate the real problems of unemployment and poverty in America; attempts to induce the private sector of the economy to expand will never take care of America's real needs. The review on Vietnam takes the form of a policy statement, indicating that the editors consider the war to be an attempt of reactionary imperialism to retain its exploitative grasp on the "third world." They allege that the South Vietnamese governments have been puppet governments and that the Vietcong is an indigenous revolutionary force.

"World Events," written in the issues reviewed by Scott Nearing, covers a variety of topics. The April 1965 issue presents statistics on American foreign investment in Latin America and discusses the destruction of USIA centers in foreign countries. Among the topics discussed are the nature of American democracy; Howard Mumford Jones' book, O Strange New World; American economic policy; and the situation in British Guiana.

Feature articles include Keith Buchanan's article defending Cambodia's present foreign and domestic policies, the debate on prospects for revolutionary action in Guiana, Chile, and Quebec (an alliance between socialists and French nationalists), and a review of the statement of the Ad Hoc Committee for the Triple Revolution (Jobs, Income, and Cybernation). George and Louise Crowley present an article on automation, in which they set forth the idea that the dissatisfied, potentially revolutionary classes of our time are the jobless and underemployed. In a later issue, comments upon this article, including one written by a Socialist Labor Party member, are presented. The Monthly Review editors criticize the article from the standpoint of Marxist thought.

It should be pointed out that the Monthly Review approves of Communist-Chinese militancy in furthering the world socialist movement, but does not, on this account, believe that the Soviet Union should simply be dismissed as a hopeless hotbed of revisionism. The Monthly Review regards the fall of Khrushchev as a healthy sign.

Editor's Comment:
The editor requested a few minor revisions of the content. He did not express disapproval of the summary as it stood, however.

National Guardian

Address: 197 East 4th Street
         New York, New York 10009
Weekly; $7.00 per year
Circulation: 28,000

Publication Started: 1948
Format: 14-page tabloid Newspaper
Issues Examined: July 31, August 7, 14, 21, 28, and September 14, 1965

The National Guardian is a weekly newspaper dealing with major political issues and current events. Foreign affairs, foreign policy, peace movements, civil rights, and poverty problems receive coverage. Although the Guardian places itself in the radical left camp and gives coverage to a variety of radical left organizations and groups, it considers itself an independent newspaper.

The war in Vietnam receives central coverage. Leopold Aragon, of the Mexican newspaper El Dia, reports that the Socialist bloc has agreed not to mediate the conflict in Vietnam and has urged negotiations between the United States and the National Liberation Front. Michael Munk points out that President Johnson does not have a "consensus" for his actions in Vietnam and claims that we are, in fact, waging a war against a whole people rather than against an enemy army. In another article, Munk maintains that the war in Vietnam will cause a "Korean economy" in the United States, which will ensure the continuation of the present boom and ameliorate the unemployment problem by absorbing many people in the draft. He also discusses Senator Wayne Morse's (D.-Ore.) statement that a national emergency may be declared by the President as a result of the Vietnam situation. Other articles on this topic include William Worthy's "South Vietnam's Patriots," a discussion of National Liberation Front policy and objectives, and Freda Cook's "North Vietnam's Strength," which reports on the progress which the North Vietnamese government is making in providing a higher standard of living for the people of North Vietnam.

The National Guardian also covers the crisis in the Dominican Republic, the separation of Singapore from Malaysia, and the commemoration of the dropping of the first atom bomb on Hiroshima. Mario Mejia Ricart discusses the case for the Dominican rebels and claims that the United States is behind General Imbert's forces, operating against the constitutionalists under the pretext of anti-Communism. William J. Pomeroy in an article subtitled "The Beginning of the Collapse of a Fraud," points out that although the separation of Singapore from Malaysia was largely caused by Chinese dissatisfaction with Malay policies it still constitutes a blow to British neo-colonialism.

Cedric Belfrage, "Editor-in Exile" in Mexico, also reports periodically on Latin American affairs: he discusses guerrilla activity in Peru and the chances for revolutionary success in the South American country.

Developments in the American peace movements receive coverage. In a "Report to the Readers" the editors of the National Guardian discuss the alignment of various groups in the peace movement, the criticisms leveled against radicalism by I. F. Stone in his weekly newsletter, and the relevance of radicalism to the peace movement. In another article, Michael Munk reports on the spread of teach-ins and demonstrations concerning the war in Vietnam to "neighborhoods" in New York City, to illustrate that the movements are not merely campus-centered. Pieter Romayn Clark describes his peace and anti-Vietnam war activities carried on as an inductee, presenting a possible course of action for those who cannot claim to be conscientious objectors and do not wish to be incarcerated. Several articles report on the Assembly of Unrepresented Peoples recently held in Washington. This Assembly declared peace in the name of those who felt they were not being represented by the U.S. Government. National Guardian reports on similar peace activities across the nation.

Grace E. Simons states that the Watts riots indicated three things: (1) the resistance of the power structure in Los Angeles to Negro demands, (2) total community involvement in the riots in the ghetto, and (3) a sharp cleavage between Negro leaders and the community. In another article, William A. Price interviews Charles R. Sims, the leader of the Bogalusa's Deacons for Defense and Justice, a Negro organization committed to the armed defense of Negro communities and civil rights workers. Sims claims that there is a definite need for the Deacons because the Southern police do not protect the rights of Negroes. A third article reports on two members of the Mississippi Freedom Democratic Party's advocating that Negroes refuse to serve in Vietnam until Mississippi is free. Patricia Brooks discusses Lowndes County, Alabama, and the murder of Jonathan Daniels in an article entitled "Lowndes County: Prelude to Murder."

Among articles dealing with domestic affairs, Grace Simons discusses the end of the bracero program, and William Price, the New York primary campaign. Price points out that radicals are beginning to enter the political arena in New York City by contesting several districts and offices.

Editor's Response:
The editor approved the description of content and considered it a fair version.

New America

Address: Room 402
1182 Broadway
New York 1, New York
Twice monthly (monthly in July and August); $4.00 per year
Circulation: 8,000

Publication Started: 1960
Format: 8-page tabloid Newspaper
Issues Examined: February 8, March 24, and April 16, 1965

New America designates itself "an official publication of the Socialist Party." The Socialist Party is a member of the Socialist International. However, the journal states that "only editorials necessarily express the official viewpoint of the Socialist Party." New America brings together a variety of views within the democratic left and contains numerous debates and exchanges of opinion on domestic and foreign policy.

The newspaper gives broad coverage of labor, political, civil rights, and international news from a democratic-socialist standpoint. On the labor front, the February 8, 1965 issue carries a story on the strike of welfare workers in New York City. It analyzes the strike and its results, especially its implications for white-collar union activity. In the same vein, the journal reports on the election in which the AFL-CIO affiliate union became the collective bargaining agent for Philadelphia teachers. A third article discusses the recent decision of the Secretary of Labor, Willard Wirtz, to limit bracero immigration into the United States and to provide minimum wage rates for agricultural workers. The article notes the results of attempts at union organization among farm workers.

Political affairs constitute a major source of topics for New America writers. Paul Feldman presents an analysis of the quandary in which the Republican Party finds itself after the Goldwater debacle. Feldman contends that those Republicans in touch with the reality of corporate interests will reject the ideological fanaticism of the ultra-right. However, "reactionary alternatives" of the ultra-right will still have some attraction as long as fundamental and outstanding problems in America are not dealt with effectively, Feldman adds. R. W. Tucker discusses the provisions of the present Medicare proposal and the opposition to this proposal. Jack Newfield's "The Battle of Albany," a discussion of the intricacies of democratic in-fighting in New York, serves as a further example of the newspaper's political analyses.

Michael Harrington contributes an article on "The Limits of the Great Society," in which he maintains that Johnson's "consensus" politics cannot and must not be allowed to eliminate the occasions for conflict arising from present, pressing, and unfulfilled demands of the poor, the Negroes, and other oppressed groups, and from the social needs of our country in general. Michael Harrington critically evaluates the poverty program and other domestic and foreign issues.

Civil rights receives coverage in "Giant Step on Freedom Road," which analyzes the events in Selma and the legislation to which they gave rise. A participant in the Selma march, Rachelle Horowitz, gives eyewitness accounts of what she saw and experienced in Alabama. In other issues, Bayard Rustin discusses the character and murder of Malcolm X and their relation to the psychology of the ghetto, the actualities of political power, and the problems of the alienation of the Negro community from the total society and vice versa.

New America devotes many columns to international affairs. Both Norman Thomas and Larry O'Connor write on the war in Vietnam, calling for negotiations and the neutralization of both Vietnams. Larry O'Connor asserts that "both power blocs" would (in such a situation) have to accept "whatever social regimes may be established by the peoples of the area themselves." Other articles on Vietnam, such as Alex Garber's "Alternatives to Vietnam War," present the view that the U.N. and its developmental agencies must be given a chance to operate in Southeast Asia. Articles state that there are a number of diverse opinions on Vietnam within the Socialist Party.

Articles appear in the March 24, 1965 issue on the congressional elections in Chile, which confirm and strengthen Christian-Democratic President Frei in his social-democratic program, and other articles discuss social unrest and opposition to Franco on the part of students and workers in Spain. In another issue, an article entitled "Germany - Twenty Years After" expresses the hope that the Social Democratic Party of Germany will help in the building of a truly democratic society in Germany, as it has in the postwar past in the Länder, where it holds power. Finally, an issue airs a controversy over "African socialism," i.e., the socialism of many "one-party states" in Africa. The controversy centers around the allegedly non-democratic character of these states and the economic prerequisites for socialism.

New America also gives some attention to university activism and educational reform.

Editor's Response:

"I think your description of New America is an excellent and a fair one. I added a few suggested comments, but they are not very important."

New Politics

Address: 507 Fifth Avenue
         New York, New York 10017
Quarterly; $3.50 per year
Circulation: 5,000

Publication Started: 1961
Format: Small size, 136-page Magazine
Issues Examined: V. 2, 1962; Vols. 1 and 2, 1963; Vol 3, No. 4, 1964; Vol. 4, No. 1, 1965

    New Politics, a "Journal of Socialist Thought," is independent of any party or organizational affiliation. The editors of the periodical express the hope that New Politics "will offer an opportunity for all socialist views from left to right to confront not only the political reality but also each other and their critics." However, democratic and non-Communist attitudes seem to prevail in the writing in New Politics, regardless of specific stances taken toward particular issues.

    New Politics covers labor and economic problems, domestic issues and international relations, generally from a theoretical point of view. Al Nash, described as a "long-time socialist," criticizes the "state of the unions" in America today. He maintains that even powerful unions have not striven seriously enough for the goals of better working conditions and industrial democracy, contending that unless a larger vision of society is held by union leaders, members will become increasingly apathetic. In another article, Burton Hall states that unionism is a "struggle to democratize the industrial regime."

    In the area of domestic issues, one article contributes to the current discussion about the nature of the civil rights movement, maintaining that the traditional radical-socialist thesis (that civil rights problems cannot be solved without fundamental changes in the economic structure of society) does not apply across the board. In some situations, civil rights and socio-economic questions can be meaningfully separated; in others, especially in the northern urban complexes, they cannot, according to the article. At any rate, the civil rights movement is claimed to have meaning and élan in itself. And another article describes the actions of the Berkeley students as "representing a landmark for the student movement and a symbol of the efficiency of mass struggle against authoritarianism."

    Several articles on international relations and foreign affairs reflect a consistent point of view. They criticize Russian "Communist-totalitarianism" and, to a certain extent, accept the idea of the "cold war." Julius Jacobson's article "Russian Law Enters the 'Final Stages of Communism'" discusses what the author considers to be extremely illiberal, arbitrary, and retrogressive aspects even in the post-Stalin legal system of the Soviet Union. An "exchange of views" on "Socialist-Communist collaboration" finds one protagonist expressing the hope that the amelioration of Russian conditions will make a reunification of Marxist thought and action, and of socialist thinkers, possible "someday"; while his opponent states that collaboration is not possible until democracy becomes a reality in the Soviet Union, the labor unions are free, and the Eastern European countries are independent.

Discussing international relations, writers in <u>New Politics</u> often stress the need for the United States to understand conditions in the world from viewpoints other than that of American military security and to view the Cold War in political rather than in military terms. They argue that a truly "democratic and anti-imperialist" foreign policy would enable us to take advantage of Russian and Chinese weaknesses. Concerning the war in Vietnam, the Winter 1965 issue contains an article stating three views of opposition to the war. Norman Thomas suggests an immediate cease-fire. Alex Garber says that not only is a cease-fire necessary, but also the recognition of Red China as a major power is necessary, and Bernard Bolitzer expresses the view that the United States should withdraw.

Apart from purely political issues, questions of interest relating to Jewish persecution receive discussion. For example, an expose of <u>Judaism without Embellishment</u>, a book published in the Ukraine, and a controversy over Hannah Arendt's book, <u>Eichmann in Jerusalem</u>, appear.

Editor's Response:
"We found your description a fair-minded one."

New World Review

Address: Suite 308
156 Fifth Avenue
New York, New York 10010
Monthly; $3.50 per year
Circulation: 7,000

Publication Started: 1932
Format: Small size, 68-page Magazine
Issues Examined: January, February, March 1965

The <u>New World Review</u> focuses primarily on life, society, and political-economic affairs in the socialist countries of Europe, particularly the Soviet Union. Only a few articles in the issues reviewed deal with other matters. In one article the editors delineate the peace tasks for the coming year: (1) to end the war in Vietnam, (2) to end the intervention in the Congo on the part of the United States and Belgium, and (3) to sign a disarmament agreement with all nations--first, for the purpose of dispensing with nuclear weapons and, second, for general disarmament and peaceful coexistence. Editorials in the February and March issues elaborate on the problems of Vietnam and the Congo, stressing the need for a more just policy on the part of the United States in relation to these conflicts. The <u>New World Review</u> features a book review section, which gives coverage to books on science, world affairs and the arts, as well as books concerned with the Soviet Union.

Covering topics not specifically concerned with the Soviet Union or Eastern Europe, Martin Hall reports on the World Peace Conference held in India in 1964, and Eslanda Robeson comments on Alex Quaison-Sackey of Ghana, the President of the 19th session of the United Nations.

Charles Allen, Jr., discussing Soviet Trade Unions and socialist approaches to labor, reveals that in Russia there is one union for an entire plant, and there are no craft unions. He maintains that the unions play a much greater role in the members' social life and that increased productivity is not considered to be inimical to the interests of the worker by his union. Reporting on Russian life, editor Jessica Smith discusses her visit to the Republic of Georgia. The natural beauty of Georgia, and its rich cultural and poetic traditions particularly impressed Miss Smith. While there, she interviewed the poet Irkali Abashidze and discussed with prominent Georgians various topics from Stalinism to the work of the famous medieval Georgian poet, Rustaveli.

The New World Review regularly presents supplements entitled "U.S. - U.S.S.R. Facts." One such supplement concentrates on the various cooperative programs in which the U.S. and the U.S.S.R. participate, and discusses areas where more cooperation is possible and those where serious barriers to mutually profitable relations exist.

On Eastern European affairs, Laszlo Boka discusses the behavior and attitude of the younger generation in Hungary. He remarks that a pattern of apparent dissatisfaction is typical of all youth and stems from a desire to fit practice to theory, a lack of patience with sham and falsehood, and a wish to develop as individuals, rather than as cogs in the machinery of society. In other articles about Eastern Europe, Lement Harris and Eleanor Wheeler report, respectively, on agriculture in East Germany and new economic trends in Czechoslovakia. Harris discusses the development of cooperative farming in East Germany after the war, remarking that within a short period of time, most of the cooperative farms will become financially independent. Miss Wheeler discusses the increasing decentralization of the Czechoslovakian economy, which is expected to result in a better response to consumer demand on the local level.

The New World Review also gives coverage to the arts, including reports on the International Ballet Competition in Bulgaria and the Leipzig film festival. It also includes reprints of articles, speeches, and stories translated from Eastern European journals.

Editor's Comment:

"We feel that your review is indeed a very fair and adequate characterization, and would like to compliment you and your assistant on this thoughtful and understanding treatment.

"There is little that I would want to suggest by way of any changes or additions.

"Our over-all coverage is somewhat broader than indicated in the first paragraph, although I am sure this is a very fair summary of the material in the particular issues reviewed. And the larger coverage is indicated to some extent in the examples of articles given.

"From our own point of view, we would like to make clear our constant and continuing interest in all questions of ending the threat of nuclear war, disarmament and peace, and our special current concern with ending the war in Vietnam. East-West relations, and particularly American-Soviet relations and matters of cultural and scientific exchange, are dealt with extensively in the magazine, as well as internal developments in the socialist countries, and in addition to the special supplement referred to (which appears bimonthly, by the way). It might also be worth mentioning, if you wish, that documentary material relating to the Soviet Union, not always accessible elsewhere, is often found in our pages.

"I hesitate to make even these suggestions, since all these matters are touched on; so it is entirely up to you whether or not to add anything along these lines."

News & Letters

Address: 8751 Grand River
        Detroit, Michigan 48204
Monthly (except during the summer);
    $1.00 per year, 10¢ per issue
Circulation: 4,000

Publication Started: 1955
Format: 8-page tabloid Newspaper
Issues Examined: May, 1965; January, 1966

News & Letters is published in Detroit by a group headed by Miss Raya Dunayevskaya, who terms herself a "Marxist-Humanist." The paper largely consists of news items and letters covering labor relations, civil rights, student activities, and foreign affairs. Articles and letters are sent in by readers throughout the country and the world. Most of the articles and columns (other than the regular two columns by intellectuals: "Two Worlds" by Raya Dunayevskaya, and "Our Life and Times" by Peter Mallory) are written by workers and youths, many of whom are Negro.

In "Worker's Journal," a regular feature, editor Charles Denby, a Negro production worker, discusses work grievances, civil rights, and current events and presents opinions on these matters of other men working in the same auto plant. In "Way of the World," another regular feature, a Negro woman gives her opinions on topical issues centered on civil rights. "Youth," a regular feature written by Eugene Walker, covers student activism, and "Our Life and Times," by Peter Mallory, covers foreign affairs, supplementing Miss Dunayevskaya's editorials.

Editor's Response:
"This 'unique combination of worker and intellectual' is an attempt to work out the unity of theory and practice, in practice--and it is this effort to unite mental and manual, thinking and doing, that we consider fundamental to our philosophy of 'Marxist-Humanism.'"

The Partisan

Address: 58 West 25th Street
         New York, New York 10010
Quarterly; $2.00 per six issues
Circulation: 2,000

Publication Started: 1965
Format: 32-page Magazine
Issues Examined: April, July, 1965

The Partisan is the magazine of the organization called Youth Against War and Fascism. An editorial in the first issue states that this organization identifies "with the force of the oppressed . . . which can be found in the rising blood pressure of a million black men and women . . . it is conspicuously present at every eviction, foreclosure, and repossession; it binds brother to brother when working men are out on strike; and it is disconcerting and somewhat frightening to the Deans of Berkeley . . . ." Youth Against War and Fascism also supports "national liberation movements" in all countries, particularly in Vietnam, and acknowledges Communist China as the world revolutionary leader.

The views and interests of Youth Against War and Fascism appear in articles such as "When You're Down and Out--Harlem, N. Y. and Monroe, N. C.," "Fighting Rats and Landlords on the Lower East Side," "Chronicle of Police Terrorism," "Pages from Revolutionary History: The Long March (of the Chinese Red Army) and Karl Liebhnecht, 'The Enemy is at Home,'" "Martyred Vietnamese Patriot," "Eye Witness China," "Albizu Campos, His Life and Struggles," "Indonesia Breaks Away," and "Lincoln Rockwell and the College Lecture Circuit."

People's World

Address: 81 Clementina Street
         San Francisco, California
         94105
Weekly; $5.00 per year
Circulation: 8,149

Publication Started: 1938 (Published daily until February, 1957)
Format: 12-page tabloid Newspaper
Issues Examined: September 18, 25, and October 2, 1965

The People's World is a Pacific coast left-wing weekly, representing a united front of Communists and other leftists. Issues reviewed cover three major topics: the situation in Vietnam, labor problems, and civil rights.

Attacking U.S. "aggression" in Vietnam, Robert Phillips in "View from North Vietnam" presents the view of the war given by Pham Van Dong, premier of the Democratic Republic of Vietnam, to two Americans who interviewed him in North Vietnam. Premier Dong asserts that North Vietnam will not escalate the war but will fight back. "Protests Mount in Bay Area against U.S. role in Vietnam" discusses the march and mass meeting planned by various peace groups in San Francisco. "Vietnam and Politics," an editorial, describes the influence of the Johnson administration's "escalation of the war" on American politics, while "Demo Group Bucks LBJ Viet Ultimatum" reviews the then unsuccessful attempt of the Governor of California to force the resignation of the President of the California Democratic Council, Simon Casady, because of the latter's criticism of the U.S. Vietnam policy.

People's World also gives considerable coverage to civil rights. Don Wheeldin in "A Negro Reporter's View of Watts' Political Impact" analyzes the impact of Governor Brown's (D.-Calif.) appointment of John A. McCone, former CIA head, to head a statewide committee to investigate the Watts tragedy. "Negro-Labor Dialogue Moves to Meet the Challenge of Watts" discusses the meeting of a committee of ten trade unionists and civil rights activists with leaders of the Los Angeles County Federation of Labor to develop a program of jobs for members of minorities. On the same topic, another article discusses the view that both labor and the civil rights movement must address themselves to the question of the provision of jobs for the Negro. "Racist Terror Grows in Dixie" presents a pattern of "creeping violence" alleged to be manifesting itself in the Deep South.

Discussing labor questions, "S. F. Press Merger Kills a Lot of Jobs" claims that the mergers of newspapers in San Francisco in order to share costs will wipe out 1,000 to 1,600 jobs. On the same subject, another article discusses the resolution of the International Typographical Union to the September meeting of the San Francisco Labor Council to act to preserve 800 jobs that would be lost and to prevent the curtailment of "service to the reading public" that would be caused by a merger.

People's World usually devotes two pages to theater, film, and book reviews, and often contains sports coverage.

Political Affairs

Address: 23 West 26th Street
        New York, New York 10010
Monthly; $5.00 per year
Circulation: 5,000

Publication Started: 1921
Format: Small size, 64-page Magazine
Issues Examined: October, November, December, 1964

Political Affairs designates itself as the "Theoretical Journal of the Communist Party, USA." It presents the party's official position on political issues, current events, and foreign affairs; it also publishes the views of leaders of other more or less Soviet-line Communist Parties of the world.

Commenting on the Presidential election in the December 1964 issue, writers praise the "united front" political tactics traditionally advocated and practiced by the CPUSA. Articles in issues before and after the election attempt to expose the ultra-right in general and Barry Goldwater in particular, in line with Gus Hall's position in his pamphlet, "The Eleventh Hour: Combat the Fascist Menace." After the Johnson victory, Political Affairs published the CPUSA line on domestic strategy, which advocates that the masses attempt to organize and force Johnson to adopt more radical platforms. The issue also contains analyses of electoral results, thus giving evidence of the Party's interest in the intricacies of the American political scene and its desire to work within that context.

Hyman Lumer in "Proletarian Internationalism and Bourgeois Nationalism" takes a strong stand against the Chinese Communist Party, accusing the Chinese of abandoning Marxism-Leninism by regarding the U.S. as the sole enemy of the Communist movement, rather than the capitalist classes of all non-Socialist countries, and by renouncing peaceful coexistence and adopting narrow nationalistic viewpoints.

Another article defends cultural exchanges with the Soviet Union and states that peaceful coexistence, which is a necessity if nuclear warfare is to be prevented does not imply, however, a relaxation of the struggle for socialism.

Statements of foreign Communist leaders include summaries of the economic, social, and political situation and prospects in France and Italy. Marcelle Rosette dwells on the strategic position of a united front of Communists and leftists in French domestic affairs while Palmire Togliatti, discussing Italy, devotes his statement to tactics for winning elections and to polemics against the Chinese. A statement of Central American Communist leaders praises Castro and the Cuban Revolution, but carefully points out that "objective" political, social, and economic conditions in their countries are such that they are not ripe for revolution yet. Herbert Aptheker contributes short statements about Eastern Europe and Soviet affairs.

Editorial statements on current events include a guarded questioning of the removal of Khrushchev. Book reviews are a regular feature of Political Affairs.

Editor's Response:
"I have looked over the brief description of the content of some recent issues of Political Affairs which you submitted, and find that it is satisfactory."

The Progressive

Address: 408 West Gorham Street
        Madison, Wisconsin 53703
Monthly; $5.00 per year
Circulation: 40,000

Publication Started: 1948 (present series)
Format: 32- to 56-page Magazine
Issues Examined: January, February, March, 1965

    The Progressive generally represents the opinions of the liberal-left in America.

    Among the many articles about the war in Vietnam, Senator George McGovern writes, in the March 1965 issue, that the Vietcong is primarily an indigenous force, and that our bombing of North Vietnam would be of no avail in a war that we have no chance of winning on the ground. In the February 1965 issue, James Wechsler discusses alleged government deception of the public and its attempted control of the news media in regard to the war in Vietnam.

    Sidney Lens, another writer on foreign affairs, shows particular concern about presumed misrepresentations of foreign governments and about American support of what he calls "non-democratic, reactionary governments," most notably in articles on Indonesia and Iran. John Hatch surveys the African situation in relation to Eastern and Western diplomatic efforts and analyzes Western and African opinion on Congolese events attempting to present the assumptions, prejudices, and lines of thought which lead to such widely-differing appraisals.

    "The Word from Washington," a regular feature, purports to give "inside" news from Capitol Hill. Senators McGovern and Nelson also contribute articles on peace activities and the abolition of the draft in recent issues.

    Expose articles about ultra-right political organizations, J. Edgar Hoover, and congressional morals are presented, while the areas of economics, cybernation, Medicare, and steel prices receive discussion from a liberal point of view.

    Milton Mayer regularly contributes to The Progressive, writing on a wide range of subjects including nonviolence, which he views as an outgrowth of religious pacifism. He points out that nonviolence used as a strategy often causes people to advocate that violence be used by law enforcement agencies, particularly in civil rights episodes.

    Book reviews also appear in The Progressive. A recent issue includes Alfred Werner's article on the art of Ludwig Meidner, a German expressionist painter of the early twentieth century.

Editor's Response:
    "I find your description a fair enough summary."

Progressive Labor

Address: G.P.O. Box 808　　　　Publication Started: 1962
　　　　Brooklyn 1, New York　　Format: 120-page Magazine
Bimonthly; $2.50　　　　　　　　Issues Examined: January, February, March, 1963; October, December, 1965; and March, April, 1966
Circulation: 9,000

　　Progressive Labor, the earliest publication of the Progressive Labor Party, was conceived for the purpose of building a Marxist-Leninist labor party in the U.S. Militant labor activity in America receives the greatest amount of coverage. The editors emphasize that the leaders of most unions have abandoned positions of opposition to the capitalist class. For example, in October 1965 it is stated concerning David Dubinsky, George Meany, and Walter Reuther, "these gentlemen of labor sold themselves to the ruling class."
　　The most recent issues of Progressive Labor deal considerably with the civil rights movement and the war in Vietnam. Concerning the riots in Los Angeles, Progressive Labor states: "The revolt of the black people in Los Angeles . . . marks the total failure of Johnson's phony 'Great Society' to provide the jobs and dignity an angry people demand." As for the South, a writer comments: "For the black people in the South, genuine freedom is impossible without utterly smashing and routing the racist stronghold in the region." All the articles on Vietnam call for immediate withdrawal. The intervention in the Dominican Republic is also criticized.
　　One writer states: "The most hated government in the world today is the government of our country." Progressive Labor sees socialism as the system which can accomplish "a new political system which satisfies the needs of most of the people in our country." Communism is described as "not subversive manipulation, not the Asian peril, but rather equality in a cooperative society, internationalism, and an end to private profit, exploitation, racism, and imperialist war."
　　In addition to the articles and editorials appearing in each issue, poetry and occasionally a short story are included.

Editor's Response:
　　"Progressive Labor magazine seeks to publish revolutionary ideas primarily in the labor, peace, black liberation, student, and cultural movements. Each issue contains articles in each of these fields as well as general articles of Marxist theory, against the war in Vietnam, etc."

SDS Bulletin

Address: 1103 East 63rd Street
        Chicago, Illinois 60637
Monthly; $3.00 per year
Circulation: 5,200

Publication Started: 1962
Format: 10- to 20-page Newsletter
Issues Examined: March, April,
    and a Special Edition, 1965

    The Bulletin of the Students for a Democratic Society (SDS), a publication intended primarily for members, concentrates on organizational activities and chapter news. Activities reported upon include SDS conventions, marches and demonstrations, and community action projects. A "special edition" of the Bulletin distributed during the last two months of 1965 deals with proposed SDS activities in relation to the war in Vietnam. SDS opposition to the war arises from views on self-determination, pacifism, the nature of the South Vietnamese government, and the undemocratic premise of the selective service, rather than on an ideological position which presumes support of the Vietcong. Chapter news includes membership and financial questions, and organizational problems.
    Theoretical discussions also appear in the Bulletin, as SDS positions and ideology have never been clearly fixed, although SDS is generally known as an exponent of the "New Left" ideas on "participatory democracy" and decentralized organizations of the oppressed, in which the people themselves make the decisions.
    The SDS Bulletin seems to have been superseded by a 4-page weekly newspaper entitled sds New Left Notes beginning with January 21, 1966 (Vol. 1, No. 1); subscription $5.00 a year.

Spark - Chispa

Address: 2929 16th Street
        San Francisco, California
Monthly; $2.00 per year ($1.00 on
    West Coast)
Circulation: 4,500

Publication Started: 1965
Format: 12-page tabloid Newspaper
Issues Examined: August, September, 1965

    Spark - Chispa, the "Western Voice for Revolution," is the West Coast monthly publication of the Progressive Labor Party. The newspaper concentrates upon topical news rather than theory or analysis, but a regular exposition of the aims of Spark--"to fight for the people of the working class and strive to be a genuine voice for the socialist revolution"--is presented in each issue. Two or three pages of the tabloid are printed in Spanish. (Chispa is Spanish for "spark.")

The issues examined give considerable coverage to labor and housing questions. For example, a report on the successful bid by some garment workers in San Francisco for union recognition, a questioning of the job provisions and hiring policies of the Bay Area Rapid Transit Construction Project, and a report on the growth of a "new and militant" union of agricultural laborers (the Farm Worker's Association) exemplify <u>Spark - Chispa</u>'s labor coverage. The journal also expresses concern for better housing conditions, as evidenced in "Blaze Destroys Home; Negligent Landlord Blamed," "Mission Tenants' Union Wins Rent Slash," and "Gestapo Methods Hide Housing Project Snafu." Civil rights also receives coverage: articles point out the "lessons of Watts"--that people <u>can</u> resist oppression but they must organize and that the "ruling class" is weaker than it appears. Other articles discuss the Deacons for Defense and Justice, an armed Negro "self-defense" organization, and reports of police brutality to Negroes. <u>Spark - Chispa</u> also presents articles on the Vietnam situation which attack "American imperialism."

<u>Editor's Response:</u>
"We think the article submitted is very good, fair, and objective."

Spartacist

Address: Box 1377, G.P.O.
         New York, New York 10001
Bimonthly; 50¢ a year
Circulation: 9,000

Publication Started: 1964
Format: Small size, 16-page Newspaper
Issues Examined: May-June, November-December, 1965

The <u>Spartacist,</u> an "organ of revolutionary Marxism," is the official journal of the Spartacist League, a Trotskyist group founded in September 1966. Initially published by the "supporters of the Revolutionary Tendency expelled from the Socialist Workers Party," the <u>Spartacist</u> accuses the Socialist Workers Party of abandoning Trotskyist positions and calls for "a revolutionary regroupment of forces within this country--such that a Leninist vanguard party of the working class will emerge."

The <u>Spartacist</u> is devoted primarily to the presentation of analyses of current events which the Left considers to be of interest. It critically assesses civil rights activity, stating that the grievances of Negroes cannot be redressed except through the efforts of an "independent party based on the needs of the Negro people and the whole working class," rather than through the machinery of the Democratic Party and the Federal Government, both of which represent the capitalist establishment. A detailed analysis of the Free Speech Movement at Berkeley arrives at a similar conclusion, stating that there can be no "free university" as long as a capitalist ruling class retains ultimate social, political, and economic control in America.

The Trotskyist positions on Stalinism--that the Soviet Union is a "deformed" bureaucratized workers' state and the Soviet bureaucracy collaborates with foreign class enemies in the name of "peaceful coexistence" in order to protect its "national-caste" interests--are applied by the Spartacist to the policies of Mao Tse Tung. In line with this view, the journal questions whether Ho Chi Minh is a truly revolutionary leader because of his relationships with Stalin and Mao and his "acquiescence" in the Geneva agreements of 1954. The Spartacist criticizes "national liberation fronts," particularly in Algeria, and mass movements based on the peasantry, as in Cuba, for their lack of Marxist doctrine and class-consciousness. However, the National Liberation Front in South Vietnam receives support.

Editor's Response:
No approval specifically expressed. However, the tone of the editor's letter reflected approval. One revision, defining the Spartacist League, was made in compliance with the editor's request.

Studies on the Left

Address: 260 West Broadway
        Room 202
        New York, New York
Bimonthly; $5.00 per year
Circulation: 4,500

Publication Started: 1960
Format: Small size, 96-page Magazine
Issues Examined: Vol. IV, Nos. 3 and 4; Vol. V, No. 1

Studies on the Left describes itself as a magazine "independent of any political organization or advocacy of a specific theoretical position. The aim is to provide a meeting place for radical scholars of all shades of conviction and doubt, wherein they can apply their academic disciplines to the relation of concepts and ideas to their roots in society." The magazine devotes itself to defining the goals of the "Radical Left" and formulating the problems facing radicals.

In "The Case for a Radical Politics," Sumner Rosen states that the real goal of radicalism should be to "restore politics as the instrument by which people participate in the design and administration of their social destinies." The magazine's writers agree that this goal is not attainable through "reform" politics, but only through radical action. In "After the Elections," the editors assert that the real problem facing radicals is not the definition of goals but the building of new movements, for at present "radicalism" has no firm roots in a class or party movement. The editors concede that they know little about the sort of constituencies upon which such a movement might be built or about the processes by which such movements are formed. The editors cite problems faced by the civil rights activists, the alienated rank and file of the labor unions, and the college students who cannot accept the society they must enter after graduation as possible sources for radical movements.

Studies gives considerable coverage to civil rights questions, discussing the problems of urban poverty in the North and the dehumanizing effects of urban renewal, which dislocates families, destroys communities, and re-segregates the Negro. Articles also discuss the fight against segregation in the South, asserting that the Federal Government has not been utilizing the Constitution, the Federal Court, and Federal Laws as fully as it should.

Studies gives particular emphasis to American policies toward Latin America, discussing the failure of the Brazilian Left to prevent a right-wing coup and the futility of the self-styled leftist Goulart's attempts to solve Brazil's economic problems. Articles draw attention to the relationship between U.S. policies and interests and Brazilian policies. In "Chile: The Dark Side of Stability," Donald Bray points to the lack of improvement in the conditions of the poor during a period of political stability; he voices the belief that stability is achieved through the power of a massive bureaucracy with a decided interest in the status quo and through concessions to right-wing interests. Another article discusses the use of terrorism by the Venezuelan Left, stating that radicals adopted guerilla tactics when they could not act politically without being jailed.

Viet-Report

Address: 133 West 72nd Street
    New York, New York 10023
Monthly, January through December; $4.00 per year
Circulation: 35,000

Publication Started: 1965
Format: 20- to 40-page Magazine
Issues Examined: January, February, and March/April, 1966

In the first issue of Viet-Report, the editorial policy is stated by the following quotation from U Thant. "I am sure that the great American people, if only they knew the true facts and the background to the developments in South Vietnam, will agree with me that further bloodshed is unnecessary . . . as you know, in times of war and of hostilities the first casualty is truth."

Viet-Report articles and editorials are centered completely around the war in Vietnam. The views are often those of the people in Vietnam, taken from interviews. The January issue contains an interview with North Vietnam's Premier Pham Van Dong, in which the premier states that the political settlement of the war can come only when the U.S. accepts his four point program. He denies that North Vietnam is controlled by the Chinese People's Republic. Also in this issue is an article by French historian Phillipe Devillers, in which he expresses the opinion that "The intervention of the U.S. in the problem of Vietnamese reunification is just as inadmissable as English intervention on the side of the Confederate South would have been in the American Civil War. Paul Rockwell writes that President Johnson has misused his power in the undertaking of the military commitment in South Vietnam. He says that there is no document that legally binds the U.S. to this position of military defense.

The February and March/April issues contain an article criticizing the Michigan State University group in South Vietnam in the late 1950's. Martin Nicolaus, author of the article, says that the group of professors was not well prepared in terms of understanding the political situation of the country. He also criticizes the group for the training given to Diem's government in police tactics.

In addition to the many articles and interviews on the various facets of the Vietnam situation, there are reviews of suggested books to bring about more understanding of why the U.S. is in Vietnam and why the U.S. should not be there. Also are occasional cartoons satirizing President Johnson.

Editor's Response:

"My basic conplaint with the 'summary' is that it is diffuse and sketchy, and represents the magazine as a rather aimless conglomerate of 'views' on the war in Vietnam. As you will see from the first four issues of <u>Viet-Report</u> sent to you, the magazine was initiated for a very specific reason: to provide documentary material, eyewitness accounts not easily available in the American press, and analyses of the origins, present conduct and foreseeable effects of the war upon the Vietnamese and upon American policy in Asia. U Thant's quote does represent our editorial policy, but it is important to add that we began convinced that the 'casualty of truth' in this war is no accident. We were, and remain, inspired by the belief that the willing escalation of the war by the Administration has been accomplished through a deliberate, if sometimes reckless misrepresentation of facts and aims. Our response is to ask our readers to catch up by making available the original documents such as the Geneva Agreements, full texts of statements by 'the other side,' first-hand reports by impartial observers or competent critics of United States policy in action. The idea was and is to prepare the way for a well-informed, effective and vocal public to call for alternatives.

"With the February issue we began to broaden our scope and shift our approach. The beginning of the three-part study of the Michigan State professors in action in Saigon, 'The Professor, The Policeman and The Peasant,' is indicative of the kind of original research into the origins of the war at home which <u>Viet-Report</u> will continue to publish. In brief, we are focusing more on the role taken by various forces--institutions, individuals, ideas--in domestic society, in making such a policy which has led to the Vietnam war possible [sic]. Our scope then embraces domestic with foreign policy; our 'test' case not just Vietnam but the entire 'underdeveloped' world which presently engages United States interests."

Weekly People

Address: 116 Nassau Street
        Brooklyn, New York 11201
Weekly; $3.00 per year
Circulation: 12,500

Publication Started: 1891
Format: 6-page Newspaper
Issues Examined: July, August, 1964

The Weekly People, the official organ of the Socialist Labor Party and the oldest continuous radical periodical in the country, advocates orthodox but democratic Marxism, especially that taught by Daniel De Leon, who joined the party quite early in its existence.

Major topics of the 1964 issues reviewed include civil rights and the forthcoming Presidential election. A headline, "The South's Crimes Reflect the Rotten Capitalist Society," sums up the Weekly People's civil rights position, that there will never be racial quality until the present capitalistic economic system is overthrown.

Discussing the election campaign, writers uphold the Marxist position that the state is a tool of the ruling class, regarding elections merely as an exchange of masters. "If Goldwater spoils the Capitalist Tweedledum-Tweedledee picture and causes greater numbers of workers to vote for Johnson out of fear, he will still serve capitalism," the weekly notes.

"Socialism Means," a regular feature, often presents De Leon's vision of socialism.

Editor's Response:
"The Weekly People is not only 'the oldest continuous radical periodical in the country'; it is, we believe, the oldest in the world.

"We ourselves shun the terms 'orthodox Marxism' and 'democratic Marxism.' Our Marxism is the Marxism of Marx--and Daniel De Leon. It is scientific Socialism. And its goal is a completely democratic society, one, that is, in which democracy will prevail in the industries and services as well as in other social relationships.

"As for elections, we do indeed hold that choosing between the Democratic and Republican candidates is choosing between Tweedledum and Tweedledee. But when your description ascribes to us the view that 'elections are merely an exchange of masters,' it invites the inference that we are contemptuous of elections as such. We are not. We participate in them. We believe that the principles of which elections are a climax open the way to a peaceful and orderly reconstruction of society.

"What the Weekly People does emphasize is complete opposition to capitalism and all its supporters, no collaboration with reform movements or any other movement that rejects the principles of scientific Socialism, and uncompromising adherence to these principles."

The Western Socialist

Address: 295 Huntington Avenue
    Room 212
    Boston, Massachusetts
    02115
Bimonthly; $1.00 per year (15 issues for $2.00)
Circulation: 3,000

Publication Started: 1933
Format: Small size, 24-page Magazine
Issues Examined: Several issues 1964-65

The Western Socialist, the "Journal of Scientific Socialism in the Western Hemisphere," is the publication of the World Socialist Party of the United States and the Socialist Party of Canada. These parties proclaim their adherence to the teachings of Marx and Engels and disclaim the validity of the writings of those who have claimed to have "developed" the writings of Marx and Engels, for example, Lenin, Daniel De Leon, and Mao Tse-Tung. They also dissociate themselves from all "reformist" and "social-democratic" parties and movements and advocate the establishment of socialism through the victory at the polls of a working class aware of its historic role as the instigator of a new classless society. Socialism means the common ownership of the means of production--production for use rather than for profit--and the abolition of the wage system. Once the working class has used the vote to take over the "machinery of government," government will aid in the socialist transformation of society, according to the magazine.

The Western Socialist applies its theoretical position to current events, as evidenced in "American Political Myths," "Will Capitalism Collapse?" and "Religion and Socialism." "Gems from American History," a regular feature, includes additional accounts of class conflict and socialist activity in the United States. Letters from readers, reports from individuals or parties, and advertisements of literature are also included in the magazine.

Editor's Response:
    "Re your summary of The Western Socialist, I can only comment with a hearty: 'Excellent!'"

The Worker

Address: Box 28
  Madison Square Station
  New York, New York 10010
Twice-weekly; $7.00 per year
Circulation: 15,000-17,000

Publication Started: 1922 (then titled The Daily Worker; changed to The Worker in 1938)
Format: 8- to 12-page tabloid Newspaper
Issues Examined: September 26, September 28, and October 25, 1965

The Worker expresses Communist views; it is published twice weekly in New York. The issues reviewed cover a variety of topics, among which the Vietnamese war, labor questions, and civil rights are prominent.

The newspaper attacks U.S. policy in Vietnam: One article, "Gov't Admits Youth Try to Evade Viet War," claims that young Americans are attempting to avoid going to fight in Vietnam, since they "do not consider it their duty to serve in a war of aggression against the Vietnamese people." Another article quotes Arthur Miller as saying that Johnson's Vietnamese policies were causing in increase in American casualties. Other articles present the positions of some foreign Communist parties on the war in Vietnam: "U.S. and Italian Communists Say U.S. Forces Must Leave Vietnam" summarizes conversations between Italian Communist Party and the CPUSA on the Vietnamese problem, while another article cites the joint declaration of the Workers Party of Vietnam and representatives of the Communist Party in France denouncing "American aggression." The newspaper reports also on campaigns to end the war in Vietnam.

Labor problems are also discussed. Three articles describe the rank and file dissatisfaction with the leaders of the United Mine Workers, which led to a wildcat strike and eventual negotiations. One article asserts that, in the negotiations, union leadership was forced to become more amenable to rank and file demands and grievances. The article "McKeesport Mill Closing Hits Town Like Bombshell" reports on the announcement by U.S. Steel that it will close its National Works at McKeesport in November unless defense contracts are negotiated. Another article reports on cutbacks in steel production and the resulting unemployment.

Discussing civil rights, two articles on a Common Council election in Detroit state that the defeat of the "racists" is the main task before the "labor-liberal-Negro" coalition. Articles assert that unless this coalition is victorious, there is danger of an "Ultra Takeover in Detroit." A final article states that while many religious and civil rights leaders expressed resentment of the acquittal of Tom Coleman, accused of the murder of a seminary student, U.S. Attorney General Katzenbach simply commented that the acquittal was "the price you have to pay for the jury system."

Editor's Response:
No approval or disapproval expressed. The editor stated that "The Worker is not an organ of the Communist Party of the U.S.A."

Workers World

Address: 46 West 21st Street
         New York, New York
Bimonthly; $2.50 per year
Circulation: Not ascertained

Publication Started: 1959
Format: 4-page tabloid Newspaper
Issues Examined: Several issues 1964-65

Workers World, a publication of the Workers World Party, supports revolutionary activities on the part of the "oppressed," giving primary coverage to the Negro equal-rights struggle and the war in Vietnam, but also covering labor grievances. In a commentary on a party statement on the Los Angeles riots printed in Workers World, the journal hails the riots as a "genuine revolutionary upsurge and a sure sign of the coming black emancipation: and calls for 'workers' solidarity with the black insurrection." Reports on organization and solidarity among the people of Watts also appear.

Concerning the war in Vietnam, the National Liberation Front and its military arm, the Vietcong, receive full support from Workers World. Articles concentrate on American war atrocities, the injustices of the draft, and anti-war activities. Trotskyist positions are expressed in Workers World, and Latin American "national liberation movements" receive support.

Young Socialist

Address: P.O. Box 471
         Cooper Station
         New York, New York
Bimonthly; $1.00 per year
Circulation: 6,000

Publication Started: 1957
Format: 24-page Magazine
Issues Examined: Several issues 1964-65

The Young Socialist, formerly a newspaper but now a bimonthly magazine, is the journal of the Young Socialist Alliance, a Trotskyist-Socialist group which "has political agreement with the Socialist Workers Party, but has no organizational ties, being totally independent and self-supporting." The issues reviewed contain two regular features: "Young Socialist Notes" which gives news of protest activities of interest to the USA; and "Young Socialist Interviews," which presents interviews of Issac Deutscher and a

"French Communist Student." The balance of the Young Socialist consists of feature articles on a variety of subjects. Editor Doug Jenness discusses "New Radicals and the Antiwar Movement," contending that the antiwar movement must remain independent of the two major political parties and pursue "independent politics," clearly seeing "the pitfalls of reformist and coalitionist policies and formulating for themselves a consistent revolutionary perspective."

Other articles include "The Truth about Santo Domingo," an assessment of the fall of Ben Bella in relation to the National Liberation Front (FLN), and "Anti-War Movement Continues to Grow." The Young Socialist also presents historical studies, such as "Reconstruction and Redemption," which presents an economic interpretation of the end of the Reconstruction period in the South. National Chairman of the Alliance states in a letter that "Over a period of time we attempt to have articles on the colonial revolution, the Afro-American struggle, Vietnam, and the antiwar movement, and the issues of the day as they concern socialists." Also, a 32-page edition is put out as the group sees the need.

Editor's Response:
"From our point of view the selective summary . . . was adequate for the aims you have in mind."

Chapter 3
MISCELLANEOUS

Age of Reason

Address: 257 West 38th Street
    New York 18, New York
Bimonthly; $5.00 per year
Circulation: 4,000

Publication Started: 1937
Format: 16-page Magazine
Issues Examined: September-October, March-April, 1965

    The Age of Reason magazine, published by the Freethinkers of America, advocates a rationalist and atheistic point of view. A few expository articles, short news items, and letters from individuals in the organization to the Age of Reason or to other periodicals comprise the content of the magazine.

    Long articles, such as "Existentialism for Freethinkers," and "I Returned from the Dead," present a rationalist viewpoint concerning the order of the world and man's place in it. These expository articles reject the concept of God as irrational, superstitious and dangerous. Short news items inform readers of a Catholic priest's attack on celibacy, the opening of two New York City Post Offices on Sunday, and a Unitarian minister's statement of agnostic beliefs. Most of these news items are quoted from other periodicals. Letters written by Mr. Lewis, the founder of the Freethinkers of America, to various individuals and organizations are often reprinted in the Age of Reason magazine.

The American Atheist: A Voice of Reason

Address: 1060 Spencer Street
    Honolulu, Hawaii 96811
Monthly; $5.00 per year
Circulation: Not ascertained

Publication Started: 1959
Format: 4-page tabloid Newspaper
Issues Examined: November, 1965 and several other issues in 1965-66

    The American Atheist: A Voice of Reason is published by The Freethought Society of America, to which Madalyn Murray, Editor-in-Chief belongs. The newspaper advocates atheism and attacks the traditional arguments for belief in God; it also attacks the church as an institution. "Sweet Land of Liberty," a regular feature, presents views on the economic and political decentralization, workers' control, direct democracy, and other anarcho-syndicalist viewpoints. In the issues reviewed, the

Vietcong is defended as a force opposing colonialism, authoritarianism, and reactionary Catholicism.

Between the Lines

Address: 7 Patton Avenue
Box 143
Princeton, New Jersey
08540
Subscriptions: Circulation Department
Newtown, Pennsylvania
18940
Semimonthly (monthly in June, July, and August); $2.50 per year
Circulation: 25,000 to 30,000

Publication Started: 1942
Format: 4-page Newsletter
Issues Examined: August 1, September 1, 15, and October 1, 1965

Between the Lines, an independent news journal, attempts to provide a deeper examination of world events free from the pressures of "political fanaticism and military extremism." Charles A. Wells, editor and publisher, asserts that "only through the Judaic-Christian concepts of truth can we avoid the violent changes inherent in war, communism and fascism."

Discussing Red China's call for a worldwide "people's war," the newsletter contends that the only means of achieving world peace is through world law. It proposes that Red China must be brought into associations of nations, including the United Nations, and states that the United States must realize that communism itself is not the major cause of war but that most wars are caused by a nationalistic revolt against the past and against historical enemies. It also attacks the American "containment policy" of 1948 which resulted in an "orgy of military expansion." It states that the United States provided the arms that India and Pakistan used against one another and that the Greeks and Turks "were both armed to the teeth with U.S. weapons." Moreover, Castro "came to power with weapons captured from the Cuban tyrant Batista whom [the U.S.] armed rather lavishly as [they] have armed every other dictator in Latin America despite the misery these men usually bring to their peoples."

In a two part feature "From the Editor's Deep South Notebook," Charles Wells discusses the many generalizations and prejudices that have barred the progress of racial justice. He questions the myth that all Southerners are die-hard degregationists and that all the Negroes in the South live in squalor with no opportunities for economic advancement, and asserts that Southern Negro slums "aren't comparable in squalor to Harlem, Chicago's South Side or Watts in Los Angeles." He also emphasizes that to understand the Negro culture and its matriarchal structure we must go back beyond the slavery period to the Negro's African origins. While the males in most African tribal structures idle in dignity, African society has always been mostly polygamous and the different wives usually economically independent. "In adapting to the economies of Western society, the Negro women, who were traditionally the traders and workers, might be expected to adjust more easily than the men," according to Wells. He adds that it is highly unfair to judge the Negro family pattern immoral because the African pattern is not monogamous and that our efforts in "race adjustments--beyond civil rights . . . should focus on superimposing the Western pattern on the African tradition."

Between the Lines also criticizes the use of violence as a tactic of foreign policy and advocates the substitution of an Asian peace force under U.N. supervision for the American troops in Vietnam.

Editor's Response:

"We would underscore (the main point of our publication) as featuring reports on trends and events that are ignored or suppressed in the usual news channels--especially those matters that pertain to war and peace, race relations, social strife, etc."

Capsule News

Address: 939 North Kenmore Street
         Arlington 1, Virginia
Monthly; $7.00 per year
Circulation: Not ascertained

Publication Started: Not ascertained
Format: 6- to 8-page Newsletter
Issues Examined: October, November, December, 1965; January, February, 1966

Capsule News describes itself as "100% Americanist, 100% Independent, 99% nonconformist, 100% for the rights of all citizens as guaranteed by the Constitution, 100% against the judiciary usurping powers and violating their oaths, and dead set against phonies, liars, grafters and stuffed shirts in public life." The editor seeks to reveal the true character of various public figures; for example, Nelson Rockefeller is a "worker in the Communist vineyard"; Drew Pearson has a "tie up with the Russian government" and performed an "espionage job . . . for them on MacArthur's troops in Korea which cost us 50,000 casualties."

The editor, Morris Bealle, opposes the "no-win" policy of the U.S. in the Vietnam war. The basis of his opposition is his belief that American oil companies perpetuate the war because of their profit from the oil business in Southeast Asia. He believes that the U.S. does not want to win the war because if "we destroyed the Vietcong Army, U.S. troops would have to be pulled out . . . then the Southeast Asian governments could claim the oil that God put under their ground, take it away from Standard and Shell.

And the Wall Street and Rockefeller Center Hogs could do nothing about it."

Capsule News reports that the L.A. riots were Communist inspired. "The holocaust was dictated from Castro's Cuba by that fugitive Negro thug Robert F. Williams in Communism's 'Radio Free Dixie' broadcasts-- as have previous (so called) civil rights disorders." The editor opposes the civil rights movement, believing that "The Civil Rights Act . . . is a license for Negro crime."

The newspaper opposes the United Nations which it refers to as a Communist "trap," and which it believes will one day bring Communist domination. It describes the Supreme Court as a "judicial junto, . . . tear[ing] the U.S. Constitution to shreds."

Each of the issues examined contains a page entitled "Washington Beat," which includes selected news items written from a conservative yet anti-capitalist position in regard to world politics. Capsule News frequently refers to "the Rockefeller Hierarchy" which it considers blamable for the war in Vietnam, the turmoil in the Congo, and the problems in the Dominican Republic.

Editor's Response:
The summary "seems to be a fair and clear description of 'Capsule News.'"

Church and State

Address: 1633 Massachusetts Avenue, N.W.
Washington, D.C. 20036
Monthly; $3.00 per year
Circulation: 200,000

Publication Started: 1948
Format: 16-page Magazine
Issues Examined: February, March, April, May, 1965

Church and State is the organ of Protestants and Other Americans United for Separation of Church and State; the magazine consists of several regular features (including editorials) plus special reports and articles. Features include "The Law in Action," "The Courts Say," "As Seen from Here," and "This Month."

Church and State gives central attention to the question of the use of public funds for the type of aid to private and parochial schools envisaged in recent Federal and state legislation. Legislation conceived of as an aid to the child rather than to the institution which the child attends is denounced as a subversion of the First Amendment respecting "establishment" and an assault on the state constitutions and laws which specifically prohibit the use of public funds for religious institutions. Church and State claims that no matter how indirect the aid might be, the use of public tax money for aid to parochial schools violates the first and fourteenth amendments to the Consititution. The magazine also takes a strong stand against public tax aid to provide transportation for children attending parochial schools.

Further problems of church-state relations arise from the Federal "war on poverty" and urban renewal programs, according to <u>Church and State</u>. The magazine maintains that under these programs public land and funds are being used to benefit churches and church organizations, especially Roman Catholic. The February 1965 cover story presents the struggle of a small evangelical-fundamentalist church to keep its land from being preempted <u>via</u> urban renewal for a Roman Catholic school.

<u>Church and State</u> advocates public programs of information and dissemination of birth control techniques and materials. The magazine also presents arguments for the taxing of church property and income that is not directly related to worship purposes. "Religious Tax-Exempt Property in Buffalo" traces the trmendous increase of nontaxable church property in Buffalo since 1900.

Church-state relations in other countries also receive coverage. "News from Far and Near," a regular feature, presents reports on activities mainly in predominantly Roman Catholic countries, especially Spain, Italy, and the Latin American nations. A long article on "The Plight of Religious Minorities in Spain" and one on church-state relations in Hong Kong are indicative of the international scope of the publication.

Editor's Response:

"I am not sure that our journal is properly classified as 'nonconformist' or 'minority opinion.' Until very recently, if indeed the case is otherwise now, most of our distinctive positions, such as a ban on public assistance to religious schools, have been supported by a majority opinion.

"I would consider the statement a fair one."

Civil Liberties

Address: 156 Fifth Avenue
      New York, New York 10010
Monthly; 50¢ per year to ACLU members
Circulation: 80,000

Publication Started: 1931
Format: 4- to 8-page Newsletter
Issues Examined: June, 1965

<u>Civil Liberties</u> is the monthly newsletter of the American Civil Liberties Union (ACLU), which is dedicated to the "preservation and strengthening of freedoms guaranteed to us under the Bill of Rights" and affirms that "these rights belong to all--without exception."

<u>Civil Liberties</u> contains articles discussing the work of the American

Liberties Union and seeks to keep ACLU members informed about their organization and its recent activities. Thus, the newsletter includes reports on ACLU court cases, legislative activities, and policy statements both for the national organization and for its 38 state affiliates.

The June 1965 issue of Civil Liberties contains articles entitled "Major Victory Won in Mail Censorship Case," "Louisiana ACLU Chairman's Car, Aide's Church Are Both Bombed," and "Landrum-Griffin Act Is Hit in ACLU Brief." The ACLU Board of Directors also publishes its policies regarding shared-time programs in the schools, the death penalty, and libel suits, in this issue.

Editor's Response:
Editor expressed no disapproval.

Destiny

Address: Merrimac, Massachusetts 01860
Monthly; $3.00 per year; foreign rate $3.50 per year
Circulation: Not available for publication

Publication Started: 1930
Format: 16- to 24-page Magazine
Issues Examined: 8th, 9th, and 10th issues, 1965

Destiny is a religious magazine which places great emphasis on Biblical prophecy, interpreting world events in the light of that prophecy. A central principle is the idea that the Anglo-Saxon-Celtic peoples constitute the House of Israel, the chosen people of God in the world today. Destiny frequently presents findings showing that the Jews are not the House of Israel. The editors believe that the House of Israel has great responsibility and is in danger if it does not fulfill it. They feel that prophecy indicates that we are living in the last times and that we are witnessing and will witness momentous events.

Destiny discusses such issues as the Vietnam war, which it opposes as a no-win war; the civil rights movement which it opposes for inciting Negroes to savagery; the U.N., which it considers fruitless; and Communist infiltration.

Each issue contains a section entitled "The March of History," which analyzes world events; various other articles, some of which are primarily religious in nature; and a "Credendum" which states Destiny's position on the modern House of Israel.

Editor's Response:
"We are pleased to extend our approval of the summary as written."

FCNL Washington Newsletter

Address: 245 Second Street, N. E.
         Washington, D.C.
Monthly; $3.00
Circulation: 17,000

Publication Started: November, 1943
Format: 4-page Newsletter
Issues Examined: June, July, and August-September, 1965

    The FCNL Washington Newsletter is a publication of the Friends Committee on National Legislation, "a committee of Friends working with like-minded persons attempting to translate Quaker beliefs into political education and action." This publication frequently emphasizes the need to "strengthen international institutions and build a world of law and order"; FCNL Washington Newsletter holds it imperative that the United States tendency toward unilateral military action be stopped. It opposes American intervention in Vietnam and Santo Domingo.

    The emphasis in FCNL Washington Newsletter is on reporting and commenting on Congressional actions, "particularly in the areas of international relations and human rights, both at home and abroad."

    "Friends Committee on National Legislation works particularly with Congress where national policy is enacted into law. It concerns itself with contributing continuous activity in interviewing legislators, with firsthand reporting on Congressional developments to its readers, and encourages letters, telegrams and visits to Congressmen when they will be most effective." This publication has the purpose of keeping people informed on Congressional action, so that they can influence its course. The emphasis is on legislation which will promote the development of a peaceful world, under law, which provides opportunities for all peoples to try to realize their full potential.

Editor's Response:
    Editor expressed no disapproval.

The Federalist

Address: 1346 Connecticut Avenue,
         N.W.
         Washington, D.C. 20036
Monthly, ten issues per year; $2.00 per year
Circulation: 20,000

Publication Started: 1954
Format: 8- to 16-page Newsletter
Issues Examined: July/August, September, October, 1965

    The Federalist expounds principles of peace through enlightened world government. As the official journal of the United World Federalists (UWF), whose motto is "World Peace Through World Law," The Federalist supports programs to strengthen the United Nations organization.

In the October 1965 issue, the journal prints excerpts from Ambassador Arthur Goldberg's address to the U.N. General Assembly after the September 22 cease-fire agreement between India and Pakistan. The Federalist comments that Goldberg's speech presents a "summation of all the ills and vulnerabilities confronting the prospect of permanent peace." Goldberg emphasizes that "the work of bringing the rule of law to the relations between sovereign states was the greatest adventure in man's history. . . . There is no alternative except the excluded one of doom for all mankind."

One issue reviewed included a pictorial feature on the UWF World Congress, meeting in June 1965. Policy statements centered about resolutions to support the UN, but the UWF also urged U.S. Senate ratification of four international conventions dealing with genocide, the abolition of slavery, the abolition of forced labor, and political rights of women.

The July/August 1965 issue contained an obituary for Adlai E. Stevenson which praises the Ambassador as "a citizen of the world" whose "elegant phrasing frequently touched a universal chord." The obituary includes excerpts from Stevenson's messages to the UN, among which is the statement that "The United World Federalists . . . has been dedicated from the beginning to the support of the United Nations, and to the belief we share that the rule of law must supplant the old and unreliable rule of force."

Another article covers a survey of UWF membership that reports the average Federalist is a member of the "exclusive elite sometimes called opinion movers," has finished postgraduate studies, earns $14,000 a year, and is 52.

Reports on prospects for peace-keeping frequently appear. The Federalist also includes short book reviews, letters to the editor, UWF organization news, and comments on certain aspects of U.S. foreign policy and international developments.

Editor's Response:
Editor expressed no disapproval.

The Independent

Address: Exposé, Inc.
    239 Park Avenue South
    New York 3, New York
Monthly; $3.00 per year
Circulation: 10,000

Publication Started: 1952
Format: 8- to 16-page tabloid Newspaper
Issues Examined: Nos. 121, 122, 124, 125, 126, and 128, 1962

The Independent, edited by Mr. Lyle Stuart, champions complete freedom of expression and of the press. Formerly entitled Exposé, The Independent retains exposé stories as one of its major features. A favorite subject seems to be the connection between cigarette smoking and lung cancer. Several articles in the issues reviewed attack misleading cigarette advertisements. The Independent also reprints medical reports on cigarette smoking. Food and drug adulterations, advertisement misrepresentation, and other unfair trade practices are frequent subjects of Stuart's expose articles.

"Censorship Corner," a regular feature, denounces all efforts at censoring or banning literature by bringing such practices to the reader's attention; it also discusses questions connected with banning and censoring pornographic literature.

Another regular feature, "Inside the Nation's Press," attempts to expose the inaccuracies or prejudices of America's major publications. It points out distortions or omissions, especially in the reporting of foreign affairs.

The balance of features in The Independent include editorial viewpoints, which generally reflect anti-colonialist, anti-imperialist, anti-clerical, and anti-fascist sentiment, and nonconformist attitudes toward sex.

In the area of anti-colonialism and anti-imperialism, Latin American affairs receive considerable coverage. Robert Taber, who wrote a book favorable to Castro's Cuba several years ago, writes articles on Latin American affairs which are severely critical of American aid and policies. He has traveled extensively in Latin America and criticizes the U.S.'s bungling actions, presenting fundamental opposition to its basic Latin American policies.

Several writers for The Independent display strong anti-clerical attitudes. George Seldes and Mason Rose write periodic features attacking the Catholic Church. However, the Soviet Union and "Communism" receive equally sharp criticism, for Seldes and Rose often write from the viewpoint of champions of freedom of thought and expression and attack those who seek to curtail these freedoms.

Stuart's articles on Spain reflect anti-fascist attitudes; he shows much concern about the rigid control of thought and expression which still prevails.

Editor's Response:
The reply received implied approval.

The Intercollegiate Review:
A Journal of Scholarship and Opinion

Address: 629 Public Ledger Building
    Philadelphia, Pennsylvania
    19106
Six times during the academic year;
    $4.00 per year
Circulation: 35,000

Publication Started: January 1965
Format: 48-page Magazine
Issues Examined: January, February/March, September, 1965

    Leaning toward conservatism in the sense of "preserving certain values," and stressing the "moral underpinnings of the free society, The Intercollegiate Review is an interdisciplinary journal devoted to studies of Western civilization in general, with an occasional emphasis upon the ways in which such studies are applicable to contemporary problems. The editorial policy is "anti-Utopian" and opposed to the facile simplistic solutions offered by the Left and the Right.

    As stated in its initial editorial, The Intercollegiate Review, by encouraging sound scholarship, "seeks to enable its readers to acquire the norms and values in each of the germane disciplines necessary toward arriving at competent judgments in social issues vital to the attainment and continuation of freedom."

    Canvassing a wide range of topics, The Intercollegiate Review includes essays on political theory, literature, philosophy, history, and economics. Included are "John Locke Revisited," by Willmoore Kendall; "Moral Presuppositions of the Free Enterprise Economy," by Karl Brandt; "History, a Revolutionary or Conservative Discipline," by Stephen J. Tonsor; "C. P. Snow's Corridors of Power Studied As an Anatomy of the Liberal Mind," by Theophilus E. M. Boll; "The Materialistic Curtain in Higher Education," by William Oliver Martin; and "Utopianism and Realism in International Relations Theory," by Robert L. Pfaltzgraff, Jr.

    The Intercollegiate Review publishes verse. Book reviews form another section of the journal. Many of these are review-essays such as Eliseo Vivas' review of Christopher Lasch's The New Radicalism in America; Donald Davidson's review of Edmund Wilson's The Bit Between My Teeth; and Wilson Schmidt's review of two works on international monetary theory. Arthur Miller's play After the Fall, Jean-Paul Sartre's The Words, and Felix Greene's Curtain of Ignorance (called "Red China Whitewashed") are examples of books receiving relatively unfavorable reviews.

    The Editorial Advisory Board of the IR includes educators in all the relevant fields: literature--Donald Davidson, Louis I. Bredvold, Thomas Molnar; philosophy--Will Herberg; political theory--Leo Strauss, Gerhart Niemeyer, Willmoore Kendall; history--Stephen J. Tonsor; economics--Karl Brandt, Gottfried Haberler, Yale Brozen, Patrick M. Boarman.

Editor's Response:
No approval or disapproval of summary expressed, except that version submitted was considered incomplete. Above version contains amplifications.

Left and Right

Address: Box 395 Cathedral Station
New York, New York 10025
3 times yearly; $2.50 per year
Circulation: 600

Publication Started: 1965
Format: Small size, 52- to 80-page Magazine
Issues Examined: Autumn, 1965; Winter, 1966

Left and Right describes itself as "a journal of libertarian thought"; the orientation of the articles is in praise of the Left--particularly the New Left which it says demonstrates "participatory democracy." In an editorial, Murray Rothkard states: "The New Left scorns statism and social reformism and aims to stimulate the people themselves to build parallel institutions outside of and confronting the State apparatus." Throughout, the New Left is esteemed above the Old Left because of its "activist and militant" policies. Also, there is a comparison drawn between the Old Right and the New Left. In an editorial from the Winter 1966 issue, the two movements are compared as both being "devoted to opposition to war and conscription through resistance to American imperialism." In the same issue, in an article discussing the New Right, it is stated that "the Right wing in America has never been distinguished for the intensity of its intellectual life . . . " and that the Right wing is devoted "to war, theocracy, the State police and racism."

Regarding the war in Vietnam, Left and Right would like "immediate U.S. withdrawal." The editors believe that war is an imperialist act of the U.S. Government and that "the sudden dispatch of more than 20,000 marines to the Dominican Republic" and the "U.S.-sponsored invasion of Cuba" are further instances of this imperialism.

Another stand taken by this journal is an opposition to the conscription laws of the U.S. In discussing this matter, each of the issues examined contains an article concerning David Mitchell's case in the Supreme Court (Mitchell was tried and convicted on charges of draft evasion and an appeal was made to the Supreme Court which ordered retrial). Also, in the Spring issue was a reprint of a speech opposing conscription made by Daniel Webster in the House of Representatives on December 9, 1814.

Editor's Response:
"While it is true that we praise the 'New Left,' this is not simply because of its 'activist and militant' policies but also because we believe it

to be enormously more in favor of individual liberty than was the Old Left, and it is this devotion to individual liberty which makes it similar to the Old Right, and why we favor both of these movements (Old Right and New Left). Therefore, your summary is seriously in error when it says that the point of our magazine is to 'praise . . . the left.' Our point is to advance the liberty of the individual, personal, political, and economic; fifteen or twenty years ago we would have been considered 'extreme Rightists'; the fact that now the selfsame views are thought to be 'extreme Left' is a reflection on the changes that have occurred in these slippery categories. Thus, our isolationist and anti-imperialist position was considered extreme-rightist and crypto-fascist twenty-five years ago, and is considered extreme-leftist and crypto-communist today. We try to adhere to principles, and let the labels fall where they may; hence the Left and Right in our title."

The Minority of One

Address: 155 Pennington Avenue
P.O. Box 544
Passaic, New Jersey 07055
Monthly; $7.00 per year
Circulation: 24,000

Publication Started: 1959
Format: 32-page Magazine
Issues Examined: December, 1965; March, April, and May, 1966

The Minority of One describes itself as "an independent monthly for an American alternative--dedicated to the eradication of all restrictions on thought." It questions the Establishment and consensus views. Frequently emphasized is the fact that it is difficult to get the truth from mass media and government officials. For example, one article seeks to show that Presidential press conferences do not reveal the President's real thoughts.

The Minority of One attempts to get at the truth behind generally accepted opinion. For example, it has carried articles questioning the Warren Commission's version of Kennedy's assassination and the attempt to present scientific evidence that more than one assassin was involved; another article seeks to show that the gas used in the Vietnam war is not non-toxic as the Pentagon has tried to convince the public.

The editor, M. S. Arnoni, identifies a conflict he sees as crucial: that between the optimistic and the pessimistic view of man. "There are those who say that it is inherent in man to be selfish and cruel, and that nothing could change this disposition. Such people dismiss every radical reform of society and every notion of justice as childish dreams." He sees this view as dominating our national policy. Many articles carried in The Minority of One express the view that U.S. policy is determined by lust for power and money rather than by any noble desire for freedom and peace.

Southeast Asia receives a major share of attention in the issues examined. Many articles are devoted to criticism of the U.S. policy in Vietnam. The various writers agree that the U.S. is guilty of aggression there under the pretext of helping the Vietnamese. Various articles on China attempt to show how the U.S. has been at fault in its relations with that country and urge the improving of those relations.

 The Minority of One discusses various other topics, such as civil rights. One writer warns of the danger that the civil rights struggle can become a fight for advantages rather than justifiable rights, and that there are black racists as well as white racists. Another article discusses the New Left, emphasizing the need for "clarity of revolutionary passion, principles, and social-esthetics" rather than aberration or purism.

 Each issue contains a section on books and literature (e.g., an article on Henry Miller and one on the theater of the absurd). Each issue also contains poetry that is relevant to the concerns of The Minority of One, satirical cartoons, letters to the editor, a list of "books received," an "As Others View It" page (consisting of news articles from foreign publications), and a "Lie Detector" section (which pairs various news articles to point out discrepancies).

 The following are summaries of other articles examined: "The Real Enemy is China" reviews our imperialistic policy in Asia, and concludes that it is really China we are attacking in Vietnam. "A Manifesto of Belief in Man" severely criticizes our Vietnam policy, comparing it to what the Nazis did; it also discusses the attitudes behind our Vietnam policy. "The Biggest (and Shortest-lived) Empire" attempts to show how the U.S. is involved all over the world in controlling other countries and influencing elections, etc; it also discusses why this cannot last. "The Bankruptcy of Dissent" attempts to show how officials like Robert Kennedy who claim to disagree with certain government policies soft-pedal their dissent, so that it is not influential; and how they do not dare to go all the way. "Inexpensive War?" attempts to show that true prosperity is incompatible with war. "Chinese Aggression--Myth or Menace" attempts to show that China is not really aggressive; rather it has prudently promoted its own interests. "Analogy with Nazis" compares our action in Vietnam with that of the Nazis, calling Johnson, McNamara, and Rusk war criminals, and mass murderers.

Editor's Response:

 "The synopsis of The Minority of One which you sent me is by far more informative and acceptable than the previous ones . . . a truly intelligent job. . . .

 "The liberalism of The Minority of One does not end at the national boundary; but, permeating our world view, it charts ethical and political restraints upon mighty America's role in the world. In challenging all nationalistic arrogance, it is the specific task of ethical Americans to challenge the nationalistic arrogance of their compatriots and authorities. Such is the voice of The Other American: against the Cold War, and for true democracy; against a prosperity rooted in militarism and conflict, and for an economy stimulated by human needs."

The New Leader

Address: American Labor Conference
    on International Affairs
    7 East 15th Street
    New York, New York 10003
Biweekly (irregular); $8.00 per year
Circulation: Not ascertained

Publication Started: 1924
Format: 32-page Magazine
Issues Examined: March 28, May 9, and 23, 1966

    The New Leader is a magazine expressing views that vary from the independent to the moderately liberal in ideology. This ideology is expressed in an article appearing in the May 23 issue, by George Field, entitled "For A Dynamic Center." Mr. Field states: "The center plays an indispensable role in the creation of what is, for all its faults, the most effective political and social system the world has yet devised." In this article he criticizes both the Right and the Left. He describes the tactics of the demonstrators opposing Vietnam policy as "the tactics of the extremist who has abandoned the normal democratic technique for securing changes in laws or policies." He blames the liberals for having contributed to the Communist infiltration because by "becoming transfixed with the menace from the far Right, they have neglected the menace from the totalitarian Left." He also criticizes the far Right and far Left for stimulating each other. "Where elements on the Left ignore the obvious dangers of totalitarian penetration, they stimulate the fantasies of Right wing extremism . . . . When elements on the Right resort to violence against the civil rights movement, they evoke counter-violence on the Left."
    The publication deals with both United States and foreign nations policies. For example the March 28 issue contains an article by Robert Lekachman entitled "A Time for Taxes." In it the author expresses the view that a tax increase is necessary if we hope to keep the programs of the Great Society going while fighting the war in Vietnam. Also in this issue were informative articles on the results of de Gaulle's denouncing his NATO obligations and on Rainer Barzel, whom the author believes to be a rising figure in German politics. Zbigniew Brezezinski expresses the view that "The concept of a joint American-Chinese neutralization of Southeast Asia . . . ignores the fundamental problems of domestic instability and internal revolutionary conflict" just as those "who propose merely stepped up military pressure as a solution to the present problem."
    The May 9 issue contains an article entitled "A Case of Political Obscenity" by Theodore Draper, that discusses the intervention into Santo Domingo by the U.S. It is the author's view that "the role played by the U.S. was . . . an historic wrong, an unmitigated indefensible wrong." Along with these types of articles, each issue also contains a section of book, movie, and theater reviews.

New University Thought

Address: 650 Merrick
        Box 7431
        Detroit, Michigan 48202
Bimonthly starting Fall 1965 throughout the academic year; 10 issues for $4.00
Circulation: 5,000

Publication Started: 1960
Format: Small size, 52-page Magazine
Issues Examined: Summer, 1963; Fall, 1963; Summer, 1965

    The articles examined in the issues of New University Thought are mainly oriented toward cultural, social, and economic problems with overtones of political concerns. The magazine claims to be "a political magazine, a scholarly journal, and a journal of opinion." The editors are students and faculty members of colleges and universities and "are from the natural and social sciences as well as the humanities."
    In the Summer 1963 issue there is an editorial concerned with the Cuban situation. It is the belief of the editors that "the entire Cuban situation has been symptomatic of a great . . . weakness of the industrialized Western societies . . . which thrown in the context of the Cold War has made a very dangerous place to live." In analyzing the Cuban crisis the editors feel that the two basic causes of the resulting situation were the "hostility and intransigence of U.S. policy towards Cuba and the decision of the Soviet Union to actively support the Castro regime." In the same issue is an article entitled "A Foreign Policy for Peace," in which writers Otto Feinstein and Max Mark see multilateral disarmament as the policy to be undertaken. They feel it can be brought about by test bans, refusal to give nuclear weapons to allies and the establishment of nuclear free zones.
    The Fall issue of 1963 has a large section on poverty and how to deal with the problem. In one article, Robert Theobald says that "the goal of full employment is dead for all practical purposes." Leon Keyserling, in another article, suggests ways to overcome poverty: improve income distribution; improve social security; and provide higher wages and farm income. The same issue contains an interview with a Negro lawyer concerning voter discrimination in the South
    The Summer 1965 editorial concerns university reaction to the war in Vietnam. The editors describe the policy in Vietnam as "ineffective and dangerous" and the policy in the Dominican Republic as "politically damaging in the long run to the interests of the U.S. . . . ."
    Each issue examined contains editorials and essays on mainly domestic problems. The international problems discussed are in terms of American foreign policy. Articles on art, films, books and movies are also included.

Editor's Response:
    Editor expressed no disapproval.

Ramparts

Address: 301 Broadway
       San Francisco, California
Monthly; $7.00 per year
Circulation: 145,000

Publication Started: 1962
Format: 80-page Magazine
Issues Examined: January, February, and April, 1966

    Ramparts' policy is to question the assumptions, the practicality, and morality of the "many spheres of influence comprising the American Establishment--the rarified worlds of American liberalism and conservatism, of self-satisfied clericalism, of governmental largesse and bureaucratic officiousness, of interlocking directorates in literature and art as well as in big business and big labor."

    Ramparts began as a magazine whose aim was to challenge traditional Roman Catholic thought, but it has broadened its concern to major social and moral issues. Primary concerns are civil rights and the war in Vietnam, the latter of which the editors oppose. For example, there have been special issues on Harlem and Selma; the February issue featured the memoirs of a former Vietnam Special Forces hero; the April issue had a major article on Michigan State University's role in supplying guns and ammunition to the Diem regime. Ramparts also has a strong literary bent, containing book reviews, fiction, poetry, or literary symposiums.

    Presently Ramparts is not "Catholic" at all; all faiths are represented on the editorial board. It is one of the more imaginatively edited magazines to appear in recent years and has made a major journalistic breakthrough in exposé type periodicals.

    Ramparts' articles combine traditional investigative reporting with intellectual analysis and a social viewpoint. It seeks to be an experiment in modern mass communications, to use the traditional "slick" methods of commercial magazines and yet to be a serious-minded and philosophically motivated publication.

    The publication's stated purpose is to "revitalize the Judeo-Christian ethic; to insure the dignity of all men by eradicating racism, poverty and other evils that degrade the human spirit; to break down the walls that divide men, and build up the things that unite them . . . . the raw force of true artistic creativity, the sublime ideas that can raise the mind and unfreeze the heart."

Editor's Response:
    Editor expressed no disapproval.

The Realist

Address: Box 379 Stuyvesant
          Station
          New York, New York 10009
Monthly; $3.00 per year
Circulation: 50,000

Publication Started: 1958
Format: 32-page Magazine
Issues Examined: Nos. 31-40 (1962); Nos. 58-59 (1965)

    The Realist's former masthead banner, "Freethought criticism and satire," aptly characterizes the magazine. No specific views on politics or society are consistently expounded; the magazine seems to present irreverent criticism of all aspects of life. However, the implicit political assumptions of many Realist writers could be considered Left-radical, in so far as the social and political status quo often serves as the butt of their "freethought criticism and satire." The Realist also includes straightforward presentations, espousing specific points of view. One article attempts to expose the FBI as a bastion of the reactionary forces in America, especially in relation to the civil rights struggle in the South. Another article defends the controversial "stall-in" which took place on the opening day of the New York World's Fair.

    Much of the writing in The Realist is highly satirical. Some of it is in the form of "straight" reporting of inherently ludicrous incidents, however. One writer satirizes the military strategy of the Pentagon stating that it is derived from comic strips and comic books. After describing an episode from a comic book and an actual military maneuver, the writer asks, "Is it not clear now that the Pentagon relies on Jungle War Stories for its military strategy in Vietnam?"

    The magazine also presents "gallows humor" about the bomb and the possibilities for survival. One article burlesques the idea of manufacturing a children's game based upon the chance for survival in a fallout shelter.

    Many articles, cartoons, and jokes about sex appear in The Realist. The publication conveys the belief that free-thinking people will inevitably discard some of the mores and values of a sexually backward and Puritanical America.

    The Realist features "impolite interviews"; interviewees include such diverse personalities as Norman Mailer and Woody Allen The April 1965 issue includes an article by Steve Allen in reply to a column by William L. Buckley with regard to U.S. Foreign Policy.

    "The Realist purports to have a large reading public composed of educated people who enjoy its humor and its avoidance of taking any position in politics."

Editor's Response:

"There is a _moral_ consistency underlying our socio-political irreverencies. (Is that a word?) It's difficult to crystallize but I suppose it's an opposition to authority-without-compassion . . . . whether on the left, the right, or the extreme middle. However, you're correct that we are, say, liberal as opposed to conservative--but not doctrinaire, nor unquestioning.

"You mention our straight reporting of inherently ludicrous incidents. The reason we often don't label these as non-satire or label satirical reporting as a hoax, or whatever, is that if a non-fictional piece can be thought of as _necessarily_ fictional, or vice-versa, then it is indeed pointing out the absurdity of our time."

Rights

Address: Emergency Civil Liberties
         Committee
         421 7th Avenue
         New York 1, New York
Monthly; $5.00 per year
Circulation: 8,000

Publication Started: 1953
Format: Small size, 32-page Magazine
Issues Examined: February, March, and June, 1965

    Rights reflects the Emergency Civil Liberties Committee's (ECLC) primary interest in questions concerning civil liberties and the implementation of the Bill of Rights. The February 1965 issue is a tribute to Alexander Meiklejohn, "champion of the First Amendment." Laurent B. Frantz explains that Meiklejohn believed that freedom of speech is a governing activity, like voting, which helps the electorate, the fourth branch of government, to keep the other three branches of the government in subordination to it. Meiklejohn's view that the Constitution and Bill of Rights formulated radical principles of government by the electorate seems to be accepted by many of those writing in _Rights_ and by most civil libertarians; Hugo L. Black and Thomas I. Emerson both indicate their acceptance of this thesis.

    Rights not only affirms principles of academic freedom but also concerns itself with relating "freedom" and "democracy" to university affairs in a larger sense. In "Criteria of Democracy," Les Colman states that a college or university is democratic if it serves students' needs, for the students are its citizens. He identifies four basic violations of campus democracy: violations of academic, political, social, and student freedoms. _Rights_ presents a sample set of ground rules for campus free speech and includes a copy of the Student Bill of Rights of the Constitution of the University of Chicago student government to illustrate specific rights that can be incorporated into formal documents governing student-administration relations. In "Organizing the Knowledge Industry," C. Clark Kissinger discusses the conflict between the "administrative elites" who "rule arbitrarily" and the students. The existence of this conflict makes such charters of rights necessary, according to Kissinger.

Frank Donner describes spying and surveillance activities on college campuses, charging that there is a considerable infringement of civil liberties by the FBI and the CIA in their zeal to gather information about students and student organizations.

Other articles discuss the House Un-American Activities Committee (HUAC), opposing appropriations of funds for the Committee and expressing disapproval of Johnson's call for HUAC investigation of the Ku Klux Klan. Rights favors investigation of the Klan but not by HUAC, which they view as operating in violation of the First Amendment's free speech clause.

In "The Affair on Highway 80," Clifford Durr expresses the opinion that the problems of the South are basically civil liberties problems and that civil rights may be subsumed under this broader category: suppression of speech, terror tactics, and attempts at red-baiting constitute dangers to the fundamental freedoms of all citizens, according to Rights.

Editor's Response:
"The description of Rights which you submit is perfectly fair as far as I can see, perhaps a little too favorable. For example, I think there should be a phrase in the description of the Meiklejohn issue to indicate that the articles are excerpts from speeches at the three memorial meetings for Dr. Meiklejohn. It would not, I am sorry to say, be fair to your readers to lead them to expect such a high level participation in future issues. Otherwise, I think the description is very good."

The Social Questions Bulletin

Address: 11 Forest Boulevard
    Ardsley, New York
Monthly; October through May and
    one summer issue
Circulation: 3,500

Publication Started: 1910
Format: 8-page Newsletter
Issues Examined: November/December, April, and May, 1965

The Social Questions Bulletin is the publication of The Methodist Federation for Social Action, an unofficial Methodist organization founded in 1907. This Federation "seeks to deepen within the Church, the sense of obligation and the opportunity to study, from the Christian point of view, social problems and their solutions and to promote social action in the spirit of Jesus. The Federation stands for the complete abolition of war. The Federation rejects the methods of the struggle for profit as the economic base for society and seeks to replace it with planning to develop a society without class or group discriminations and privileges. In seeking these objectives, the Federation does not commit its members to any specific program, but remains an inspirational and educational agency, proposing social changes by democratic decisions, not by violence."

This then is a liberal publication. Its concern is with political and social issues rather than with explicitly religious issues. The Social Questions Bulletin is sympathetic toward the civil rights movement; it is in favor of disarmament, the World Peace Congress, and the United Nations. It is opposed to the war in Vietnam, the American intervention in the Dominican Republic, War Hawks, and President Johnson's doctrine of "McCarthyism in foreign policy."

The Bulletin says that "anti-Communist foreign policy is sterile." It also says that "If there is not enough pressure put on the President to get him to adopt a flexible and constitutional attitude toward the increasingly dangerous Vietnamese situation, the outlook for averting a major war in Asia is indeed pessimistic."

The Social Questions Bulletin is for "patriotism that does not go along uncritically with everything that the government may do, but commends whatever is right and condemns what is wrong."

Editor's Response:
"I think the summary is very good!"

Towards Anarchism

Address: P.O. Box 261
   Cooper Station
   New York, New York 10003
Quarterly; 10¢ per copy
Circulation: 2,500

Publication Started: 1955 (Nos. 1 - 49 entitled Views & Comments)
Format: Small size, 32-page Magazine
Issues Examined: Spring, Summer, Winter, 1965

Towards Anarchism, published by the Libertarian League, an affiliate of the International Anarchist Movement, presents anarcho-syndicalist "views and comments." There seem to be no regular features or columns in Towards Anarchism; however, reports on the activities, and expositions of anarcho-syndicalist theory generally comprise a great proportion of the content. Recent issues report on the political persecution of anarchists in Cuba. Articles also comment on a presumed resurgence of rank and file militancy on questions of workers' control and relate traditional anarcho-syndicalist theories to the question of automation. They reaffirm the necessity of abolishing the state, rejecting authoritarianism in legal and moral matters and establishing decentralized production and social communes.

The magazine also includes book reviews and advertisements for literature published or distributed by the Libertarian League.

World News & Comments

Address: P.O. Box 817
        Sausolito, California
Weekly; $6.00 per year
Circulation: 3,500

Publication Started: 1962
Format: 4-page Newsletter
Issues Examined: July 26 and August 2, 1965; May 2, 1966

William Winter Comments (formerly World News & Comments) is an independent periodical which seeks to "evaluate new government leaders not by whether they are 'pro-American' or 'anti-Communist' but whether their own people live contented under their rule. We shall continue to be unconcerned by whether regimes are dedicated to Communism, Socialism, or Capitalism. Labels will never guide our thinking. The barometer must always be whether the people are better off."

With respect to Liberalism and Conservatism, the editor says: "We shall continue to be Liberal in the face of the welter of Conservatism espoused on the air and in the press. We feel there are basically two kinds of people: those who are interested primarily in themselves, their rights, interests, property, and welfare, which is Conservatism; the other kind of people are those who are concerned about others, the rights, interests, welfare, ideas and desires of other people which is our definition of Liberalism."

This periodical lobbies for a more rational approach to international relations . . . stating, for example, that problems in Vietnam cannot be solved militarily. The Vietnam war, dubbed "McNamara's War," comes under sharp attack as does the theory of the "preventive war" with China based on the "domino theory," which the author claims to have "absolutely no foundation in reality." The journal states that "only the American military people clamor for war" while the rest of the people "rub their sleepy eyes." (Mark Twain)

The newsletter reports on the growth of militant nationalism in West Germany and states that "there is a new 'national Democratic Party' which seems to be a neo-Fascist group, devoted to super-patriotism and ultra-nationalism." According to Comments six out of the eighteen top leaders of the party are known Nazis. The publication states further that what is regarded in the United States as the "Communist Conspiracy" is a "punctured myth" as Communists do not agree among themselves.

Comments advocates preventing the spread of nuclear weapons although it sees dim prospects for disarmament as long as President Johnson is committed to war in Vietnam, and China is building her nuclear power.

Editor's Response:
    " . . . the weekly publication is intended to offer a review, along with background, of significant current world events, along with editorial comment, quotes from newspapers around the world, along with specially prepared maps and special features."

Chapter 4
PACIFIST

CNVA Bulletin

Address: 5 Beekman Street
    Room 1033
    New York, New York 10038
Once a month or as needed; $2.00
    per year
Circulation: 8,000

Publication Started: 1960
Format: 4- to 12-page Newsletter
Issues Examined: May 28 and July 9, 1965

    This Bulletin reports on the activities of the Committee for Nonviolent Action (CNVA), a group dedicated to working for world peace and committed to a nonviolent philosophy. The Committee encourages nonviolent, direct action for the cause of peace; it also advocates the use of civil disobedience, both for tactical purposes and also in cases where one feels that a higher moral law demands that one disobey a more mundane law. The Committee believes in trying to convert people to its point of view through discussion. When confronting its opponents with a dedicated and sincere opposition to violent actions, the Committee attempts to engage the opponent in a dialogue. In particular, CNVA advocates that young men refuse to serve in the army, preferably as conscientious objectors, and has circulated a "Declaration of Conscience," which states that the signer will not take part in the war in Vietnam and advocates that others withhold their support for the war by not serving in the armed forces.

Editor's Response:
    "The summary is quite accurate."

Fellowship

Address: Box 271
    Nyack, New York
Monthly; $4.00 per year
Circulation: 10,200

Publication Started: 1934
Format: Magazine averaging 32
    pages
Issues Examined: May, July, and
    September, 1965

    Fellowship is the monthly magazine of the Fellowship of Reconciliation (FOR), an organization composed of men and women "who recognize the essential unity of mankind and have joined together to explore the power of love and truth for resolving human conflict." Issues reviewed concentrate upon the exploration of a single platform related to peace; they also contain two regular features, "In Context" and "News of the World of Peace."

"In Context" contains "editorial comments on the current scene." A comment on U.S. policy in the Dominican Republic claims that the constitution which the United States wants the Dominican Republic to adopt would not provide for some important freedoms. Editorial comment on Vietnam states that U.S. policies will not bring about desired results; those desiring peace should try to bring "their best perceptions" to bear on the relative claims of both sides and not pardon violence on either side.

The "News of the World of Peace" covers the activities of the FOR and of other people and groups working for peace. The article "Joan Baez Starts Nonviolent Institute" discusses the aims of this institute: "to understand the nature, principles, and assumptions of nonviolence." Another item describes the Citizens Exchange Corps, a newly-formed organization which sponsored the trip of a group of "good-will ambassadors" from America to the U.S.S.R. In the issues reviewed, this column also covers the proceedings of the FOR's National Council meeting.

"Moral and Technological Implications of Peace on Earth," the theme of the May 1965 issue, includes Robert Hamil's article, "Machine: Promise or Threat," which claims that automation can be of benefit to man, if man uses his freedom and liberation from drudgery to devote more time to the service of humanity.

In "One Man's War on School Segregation," Edward Gottlieb discusses his motives for leading a fast by teachers and school principals in order to integrate a Harlem school; the article appears in an issue dedicated to "The Quiet Battle for Peace and Justice."

"Ways Out of Vietnam" serves as the theme of the September 1965 issue. Representative George Brown in "Peace by Finesse" explains how an establishment of Zones of Peace (in which each nation would pledge strict neutrality in the cold war) would enable underdeveloped countries to implement needed reforms and free expenditures on defense for development projects. He argues that this approach could offer a permanent solution to the Vietnam problem, which would be acceptable to all.

Editor's Response:

"The description of the magazine and its content as prepared by your assistant seemed to be well done, and I would not wish to change anything.

"I might say by way of private comment, that while the magazine is an official publication of a pacifist organization, it endeavors to present to its readers a wide spectrum of comment on the issues of peace and nonviolence, and invites dissent from these positions."

Four Lights

Address: 2006 Walnut Street
    Philadelphia, Pennsylvania
    19103
Monthly (except August and September); $2.00 per year
Circulation: 9,000

Publication Started: 1941
Format: 4-page Newsletter
Issues Examined: May, June, and October, 1965

Four Lights, the publication of the U.S. Section of the Women's International League for Peace and Freedom (WILPF), reports on the activities of the WILPF and of its members. The 50th Anniversary Congress of the WILPF at the Hague in 1965 received considerable coverage. Articles also reported on WILPF activity in Selma, Alabama, and emphasized the fact that many members of the WILPF took part in the April March on Washington sponsored by the Students for a Democratic Society. Four Lights also presents WILPF positions on foreign and domestic policy and current lobbying stands. A special article on the Dirksen amendment, which would allow states to take into consideration factors other than population when making legislative apportionments, appeared in one issue reviewed. The WILPF also advocates working for peace through international disarmament, nuclear non-proliferation, and treaties, a "political and diplomatic" solution to the war in Vietnam, and cooperation through the United Nations and other channels by all nations to further social and economic development. A regular feature of Four Lights, its "Literature Corner," advertises many brochures, books, kits, and other educational materials.

Editor's Response:
    "The summary . . . seems to me to give a good idea of our newsletter."

News Notes (Central Committee for Conscientious Objectors)

Address: 2006 Walnut Street
    Philadelphia, Pennsylvania
    19103
Bimonthly; Free (contributions requested)
Circulation: 10,000

Publication Started: 1949
Format: 4-page Newsletter
Issues Examined: November/December and September/October, 1964; January/February, March/April, May/June, July/August, 1965

News Notes of the Central Committee for Conscientious Objectors presents information concerning the status and viewpoints of conscientious objectors, including noncooperators, in regard to the Selective Service. From five to ten short articles on individual conscientious objectors appear in each issue. Two regular features, "Briefly Noted" and "The Court Reporter" contain, respectively, short items of general news about pacifist and anti-draft activities and lists of those sentenced, arrested, or currently serving jail terms. From time to time important issues for draft-age men, such as the recent Supreme Court decision broadening the concept of "belief in a Supreme Being," or changes in Selective Service policies, are discussed in News Notes.

Editor's Response:
Editor expressed no disapproval.

Peace

Address: Box 139 Murray Hill
New York, New York 10016
Quarterly; $2.00 per year
Circulation: 800

Publication Started: 1963
Format: Small size Magazine with approximately 28 pages
Issues Examined: Fall, 1964; Spring, 1965

Peace is published quarterly by the American Pax Association, "an association of Catholics and others who seek to promote peace and to encourage the practical application of Christian principles to the question of war."

Each issue of Peace contains two or more major articles and a section entitled "Pax Communiques," which contains short reviews of peace activities around the world. Peace also includes editorial comment and regularly reviews books relating to war and peace. The Fall 1964 issue contains "Christian Conscience and War Today," by Archbishop Thomas D. Roberts, S.J., who discusses the Catholic Church's attitude toward conscientious objection; he advocates freedom of conscience. "Disarmament and the War on Poverty," by Professor Seymour Melman, contends that the dependence of the American economy on defense spending means that any reduction in defense spending would result in widespread unemployment. Such unemployment could not be offset by a "war on poverty" that does not attempt to generate useful civilian work under government contract.

The Spring 1965 issue is devoted to a report on Selma. "Turning Point in Selma," an editorial, compares the Selma-Montgomery march to a march led by Gandhi in India 36 years ago, stating that both marches are said to be symbolic and to have stirred the conscience of a nation. The issue also includes a review of Norman St. John-Stevas' book The Right to Life, which discusses questions of abortion, euthanasia, suicide, capital

punishment and modern warfare.
Other issues feature ROTC and "Warmongering in American Catholicism."

Editor's Response:
"We find the description of the PAX Quarterly PEACE well done."

Peace Action

Address: 144 Constitution Avenue,
   N.E.
   Washington, D.C. 20002
Monthly (June/July and August/September combined); $2.00 per year
Circulation: 1,400

Publication Started: 1936
Format: 4-page Newsletter
Issues Examined: January, March, April, June/July, 1965

Peace Action, "Voice of Peace from the Nation's Capital," exhorts Americans to press for negotiations over Vietnam and attacks U.S. violations of international law. The journal also presses for recognition of Red China and negotiation with her in our efforts to seek world peace.

In one issue reviewed Peace Action reprinted a letter to President Johnson signed by 2,500 clergymen asking him to reverse the course of American action in Vietnam. Other articles and letters press for making use of the United Nations and another Geneva Conference to mediate the dispute.

The publication also presents articles on international programs relating to the furthering of peace. Peace Action includes a story on the official inauguration of the University of Peace in Huy, Belgium; a report on an international literacy seminar; and an article on the shipment of baby chicks to Burundi by Heifer Project Inc. Advertisements for books and pamphlets appear as well as reprints of articles from other journals. A regular column, "The Good News of Peace," reports on peace missions around the world.

The Peacemaker

Address: 10208 Sylvan Avenue (Gano)
   Cincinnati, Ohio 45241
Published "every three weeks or as activity demands"; $3.00 per year
Circulation: 2,500

Publication Started: 1948
Format: 8-page Newsletter
Issues Examined: August 14, September 11, November 6, 1965

The Peacemaker is published in Cincinnati as the organ of the

Peacemaker movement, "committed to the philosophy of nonviolence and advocating civil disobedience." The newsletter reports on organizational activities, peace movement activities in general, and the tactics and philosophies of radical peace groups. It advocates noncooperation with the draft, conscientious objection and refusing to report for induction for military service. Many articles in The Peacemaker are in fact letters from men serving jail sentences for refusing to serve in the armed forces and from others who refuse to cooperate with the draft. The Peacemaker favors not posting bail or paying fines in cases of arrest for anti-war activities because one should not give financial support to a system that produces war. The newsletter also deals with matters concerning oppression and publishes articles discussing the challenge to Mississippi Congressmen by the Mississippi Freedom Democratic Party and the problems of apartheid in South Africa.

Editor's Response:
"It is a very good description of The Peacemaker."

The Reporter for Conscience' Sake

Address: 550 Washington Building
15th and New York Avenue, N.W.
Washington, D.C. 20005
Monthly (except September); $1.00 per year
Circulation: 5,000

Publication Started: 1942 (not published between September 1947 and October 1948)
Format: 4-page Newsletter
Issues Examined: May, June, and August, 1965

The Reporter for Conscience' Sake is published by the National Service Board for Religious Objectors, an organization founded at the outbreak of World War II by the churches in the interest of all conscientious objectors, with the "historic peace churches" (Quakers, Mennonites and Brethren) taking the lead in the original organization. The Reporter publishes editorial comments, articles concerning conscientious objection, and news about individual objectors. Articles have included topics such as the status of CO's in the Netherlands, a controversy concerning conscientious objection in Italy, information and comments on proposed changes in the current draft law, alternate service work projects, and the implications of the 1965 Supreme Court decision in the Daniel A. Seeger case, in which the belief in a "Supreme Being" as a basis for conscientious objection was clarified to embrace all religions, but to exclude merely political, sociological or philosophical views.

Editor's Response:
Above description was approved by the editor.

Sane World

Address: 17 East 45th Street
        New York, New York 10017
Monthly; $3.00 per year
Circulation: 20,000

Publication Started: 1961
Format: 4-page Newsletter
Issues Examined: June, July, August, 1965

Sane World, published by the Committee for a Sane Nuclear Policy, describes itself as "a newsletter of action on disarmament and the peace race." The Committee is devoted to ending the arms race and eliminating war as a policy instrument, and "supports universal controlled disarmament and a United Nations strong enough to keep peace in a disarmed world."

Sane World reports on Sane's activities and on significant events in the sphere of international affairs and peace, including the U.N. debates on nuclear proliferation. The bulletin also discusses issues of war and peace, disarmament, and the effects of war on other vital issues in the United States, including civil rights. Sane World is currently preoccupied with "the U.S. policies of intervention in Vietnam and the Dominican Republic" which it opposes, and with "immersion in the current political campaigns." Sane is not in favor of civil disobedience, nor does it favor noncooperation with the draft.

Editor's Response:
"The statement is a fair one, although not very crisply drawn." Some additions have been made as per editor's suggestions.

Student Peace Union Bulletin

Address: 5 Beekman Street
        New York, New York 10038
Monthly; $2.00 per year
Circulation: 2,000

Publication Started: 1959
Format: 8-page Newsletter
Issues Examined: April, 1964; September/October, 1965

The SPU Bulletin is the publication of the Student Peace Union, an organization centered on college campuses throughout the country, committed to peace and nonviolence. This organization supports the view that international disputes cannot be effectively settled by war and that militarism is inimical to freedom and survival. Its membership is both pacifist and

-86-

non-pacifist. The SPU attempts to educate young people in pacifism and conscientious objection, to get them involved in programs to end the arms race, and to seek alternatives to war. The publication discusses questions of war and peace and analyzes specific volatile situations. It reports on peace activities throughout the country. The SPU champions direct action, but nevertheless puts great emphasis on its educational role. In the issues reviewed there is no mention of civil disobedience, nor any advocacy of noncooperation with the draft.

Editor's Response:
The editor expressed no disapproval. He suggested a few additions, which were incorporated in the text of the summary.

War/Peace Report

Address: 300 East 46th Street
        New York, New York 10017
Monthly; $5.00 per year
Circulation: 6,500

Publication Started: 1961
Format: 20-page Magazine
Issues Examined: June, July, and August, 1965

War/Peace Report, presenting "fact and opinion on progress toward a world of law and order," discusses international affairs and their relation to peacekeeping efforts.

Articles on foreign affairs are devoted to such topics as "Communism and Democracy in the Dominican Republic" (by Juan Bosch), an analysis of current Soviet attitudes concerning the war in Vietnam and their commitment to North Vietnam, and a report on efforts being made toward the creation of a nuclear-free zone in Latin America. Other articles discuss questions of peace and world order. "The Future of the U.N." and "Whither the UN?" analyze the problems and prospects of the United Nations. The journal presents positions of the "near-nuclear" countries in regard to the activities of the U.N. Disarmament Commission. James Rosenberg discusses "A Way to Bring Life to the World Court."

Two regular features are: "On the Peace Front," which gives news items concerning peace activities, including SANE rallies and a meeting of members of Women Strike for Peace with Vietnamese women, and "Listening Post" which regularly reviews books. Several editorials appear in each issue. Issues reviewed advocated American recognition of the National Liberation Front and a negotiated end of the Vietnamese war.

Editor's Response:
The editors wished additional comments added, a selection from which follows:
"War/Peace Report is the only American magazine devoted solely to

the peace question. Discussions focus on disarmament, the United Nations, the growth of world law, and world crisis areas.

"War/Peace Report deals with both the short-term crises and the long-term problems of peace and world order. Vietnam is given an up-to-date analysis in every issue. In a recent issue sharply divergent perspectives of the Vietnam War and the problems in Southeast Asia are presented. Wilfred Burchett, writing from a pro-Communist viewpoint, tells why Hanoi rejects "unconditional negotiations," while Hans Morgenthau concludes that the main problem is not communism, but the maintenance of a balance of power with China. In the same issue, Amrom Katz of the RAND Corporation suggests that from Vietnam the U.S. may learn techniques for dealing with wars of national liberation. Other trouble spots, such as found in the Dominican Republic and Africa, are dealt with as they develop.

"Among the long-term problems dealt with are the U.N., especially its peacekeeping and financial problems, disarmament, with regular reports from Geneva and U.N. headquarters; economic planning for disarmament and defense cutbacks, and the development of world legal institutions, such as the World Court. War/Peace Report has made its pages a forum for the debate over U.S. policy toward China. On many of these questions, direct dialogues between spokesmen of the East and West are presented.

"Editorially, War/Peace Report questions Administration policies and proposes new possibilities in U.S. relations toward Vietnam, China, the Dominican Republic and the African States. On the Vietnam issue War/Peace Report advocates American recognition of the National Liberation Front and a negotiated end to the Vietnamese War."

WRL News

Address: 5 Beekman Street
         New York, New York 10038
Bimonthly; no subscription rate given
Circulation: 8,000

Publication Started: During 1940's
Format: 4-page Newsletter
Issues Examined: March/April, May/June, July/August, 1965; May/June, 1966

The WRL News is published by the War Resisters League, a pacifist organization committed to the use of nonviolent, direct action to correct the social ills of society and to end war. The bulletin carries news of peace activities and presents articles dealing with philosophical issues of war and peace. It analyzes the volatile political situations, particularly in the area of foreign relations, and supports civil disobedience. The War Resisters League sponsors the "Declaration of Conscience," which advocates that young men refuse to serve in the armed forces.

Editor's Response:
    Editor expressed no disapproval.

Chapter 5

RACE-ORIENTED

The Citizen

Address: 315-25 Plaza Building　　Publication Started: 1955
　　　　　Jackson, Mississippi 39201　(title was then Citizen Council)
Monthly; $3.00 per year　　　　　　Format: Small size, 16-to 32-page
Circulation: 40,000　　　　　　　　Magazine
　　　　　　　　　　　　　　　　　Issues Examined: December, 1965,
　　　　　　　　　　　　　　　　　　January and February, 1966

　　The Citizen is the "official journal of the Citizens' Councils of America." The Citizens' Councils have a five point program, which is: "1. Prevent race mixing; 2. Avoid violence; 3. Maintain and restore legal segregation; 4. Defend States' Rights; and 5. Correct the Court and Congress." The views that appear in the articles follow this program.
　　For example, in the January 1966 issue, an article by W. J. Simmons entitled "Political and Social Implication of the 'Civil Rights' Crisis," states that "the presence of substantial numbers of Negroes in the U.S. has always been and is today the single most divisive factor in our country." Simmons includes a quotation from Abraham Lincoln stating: "There is a physical difference between the white and black races which will ever forbid the two races living together on terms of social and political equality." Mr. Simmons also states that the 14th Amendment, which gives Negroes civil - meaning legal - right, "was never legally submitted or adopted." He quotes Thadeus Stevens as saying "It covers only civil rights... it does not touch on social and political rights."
　　In the February issue, Roy Harris, president of the Citizens' Councils states that "there must be no assimilation of the white and Negro races, either peacefully or otherwise, in this country." This same issue is devoted to a discussion of desegregated education. It is stated that "we cannot have complete desegregation and quality education." To counteract desegregated education, private education is seen as the answer because "in providing for the proper education of our young people, we provide for the survival of our race."
　　The publication opposes the civil rights movement for another reason: like the Vietnam anti-war protests, it is "Communist inspired, agitated and promoted." This quotation comes from a speech made by Representative John Bell Williams, of Mississippi, which appeared in the December 1965 issue. The publication is also opposed to the National Council of Churches as being part of the "Liberal Establishment," and aid to dependent children for the reason that illegitimacy is "accelerated by the welfare state."

Editor's Response:
　　"The summary is accurate, as far as it goes. Among others, a major point we have made that I think merits inclusion in the summary concerns

the increasing identification of the Negro Revolution in the United States with the rise of Black Power in Africa. The merging of these two revolutionary streams has been proclaimed by Negro "civil rights" leaders themselves. The resulting merger is characterized by an extreme racist anti-white foreign policy of the controlling "Liberal Establishment." Thus, U.S. policy is to destroy the legally constituted parliamentary white governments of pro-Western, stable South Africa and Rhodesia where blacks enjoy full civil rights; while at the same time U.S. policy is to aid the de facto black dictatorships of pro-Communist, unstable Nigeria, Congo, Zambia, Tanzania, etc. where whites enjoy no civil rights. Domestically, this anti-white bias is reflected in the twisting of "civil rights" into the compelling of whites to make themselves available as facilities for blacks to mix with.

"P.S. We do not oppose aid to dependent children per se. We do, however, regret the abuses that have caused this humanitarian program to become, in effect, a subsidy for illegitimacy in some localities."

Common Sense

Address: 530 Chestnut Street
         Union, New Jersey 07083
Semimonthly (monthly in July and Aug.); $3.00 per year
Circulation: Not ascertained

Publication Started: 1946
Format: 4-page tabloid Newspaper
Issues Examined: July, Nov. 15, Dec. 1, and Dec. 15, 1965

Common Sense is a "Christian" journal dedicated to fighting "Communist Internationalism." Articles express condemnation of international organizations, including the United Nations, and state that by entering World War II, America "put Stalin in the saddle" and furthered the advance of world Communism.

Common Sense questions the "'wisdom' of recent actions of the Ecumenical Council," and warns Catholics against "Judaising" their religion, in an article entitled "Jewish Proselytizing through Hillel Centers."

In "A Proud Nation Defends its Rights, Rhodesia Freeing itself from Fetters of Liberalism," Common Sense reprints an article from a British journal and expresses support of Ian Smith's government. The newspaper also expresses the view that the civil rights movement "is a perfect example of Communist strategy and Communist tactics at work."

Common Sense also includes recommendations of books expressing anti-internationalist points of view.

Editor's Response:
No approval or disapproval of summary specifically expressed. No comments, no signature. However, phrases or statements in the summary referring to the journal's vigorous advocacy of antisemitism and support of the Ku Klux Klan were crossed out and have, therefore, been deleted.

The Councilor

Address: 1827 Texas Avenue
        Shreveport, Louisiana 71102
Semimonthly; $2.00 per year
Circulation: 213,500

Publication Started: 1959
Format: 4-to 8-page tabloid Newspaper
Issues Examined: Nov. 30, Dec. 15, Dec. 30, 1965, and Jan. 15, 1966

    The Councilor is a segregationist newspaper published in the South and claims to be "probably the largest of the 'right wing' publications in America." Each issue includes some world news, but the majority of the articles concern the Negro problem in the South. A central theme in the paper is the death of whites caused by Negroes and the fact that these deaths are not well publicized. "More whites die... at the hands of Negro attacks than the total number of civil rights workers who have died from all causes in the South."
    In a description of the United Nations, it was stated that the political programs of the U.N. "lean toward Communism"; and in describing the Democratic party it was said that it was the "party which in 1936 and ever since has approved more terror by Union guerillas everywhere."
    Each of the issues examined contains a column by Westbrook Pegler in which he condemns the new reporters as setting "unusually low standards for themselves"; he calls Henry Wallace "Bubblehead Wallace"; and he condemns Eisenhower for his failure to back Joe McCarthy. Also editorials by Ned Touchstone appear with tones of anti-communism, anti-integration and anti-left. In an article in the January 15, 1966 issue, Touchstone describes the Great Society as a "Cruel Society" and a "Hate Society." Pictures that back up their views, particularly in the area of anti-integration and anti-communism, are frequently used. One issue, November 30, 1965, contains a cartoon describing the National Council of Churches as an "apostasy of subversive activities."

Editor's Response:
    "By today's standards and improper word usage, your analysis is eminently fair. If I were writing this analysis, I would use more appropriate terms, e.g., where you describe my writing as 'anti-Communist, anti-integration and anti-Left,' you have made misuse of the English language even with its Americanization. I am PRO-Constitution, PRO-racial integrity and PRO-truth. I have never, and will never, be anti-anything to the exclusion of my strong support FOR the values which were supported by George Washington and honorable Americans in the days to present.
    "I write these things with full appreciation of the difficulties of word choice in the task that you have chosen for yourselves..."
    "The Councilor is the only newspaper in the U.S. which advertises that each article it prints is absolutely true, and is further prepared to prove its veracity in court if necessary. We have never been sued for libel, and we doubt that a fair-minded jury could ever find us guilty of libel because of our practice of complete honesty which the A.P. and most daily newspapers proveable do not share."

The Cross and the Flag

Address: P.O. Box 27895
     Los Angeles, California
     90027
Monthly; $2.00 per year
Circulation: 34,000-40,000

Publication Started: 1942
Format: 36-page Magazine
Issues Examined: November, December 1964, and January 1965

The Cross and the Flag, the official organ of the Christian Nationalist Crusade, is published by Gerald L. K. Smith and always contains some material contributed by him. He usually writes one signed article and a column of editorial opinion entitled "Smith Missiles." Articles discussing religious questions include a proof of the existence of God by the "argument from design," and an assertion that the Christian institutions of America and the Christian character of civilization are about to be destroyed by a "treasonable Supreme Court controlled by Socialists, pro-Communist and even anti-Christ elements."

Smith strongly fears that the Supreme Court would sanction the taxing of church property. He praises Barry Goldwater's integrity and principles, asserting that the Republican Party, through Goldwater's influence, has become a white, Christian party; Smith expresses the hope that it will remain this way and serve as a vehicle for uncompromising conservative political activity.

Articles by other authors include a defense of segregation, written by a Southern college professor and a reproof of the Supreme Court by a Member of the California Bar Association, who attacks the decisions on reapportionment and desegregation. Warren Jefferson Davis, a lawyer, maintains that the Court is attempting to establish a Socialist tyranny over the United States.

The "Editorial Briefs" cover a variety of subjects, upholding racial integrity, white civilization, Christianity, and conservative economic and political policies and attacking organized Jewry, Communism, and integration. The column asserts that the Right in this country should not be afraid to attack the Jews, as there is ample evidence for the continued existence of a "Marxist-Jewish Conspiracy." The journal accepts the Protocols of the Elders of Zion, forged "documents" of Jewish conspiracy in the Russian Revolution, as factual evidence. The column also attacks the National Council of Churches for its liberalism and criticizes proposed liberalization of American immigration laws. The editorials praise Nasser for his resistance to Zionism and for fighting a "two-headed monster, Jew-controlled imperialism and Moscow-controlled Communism." Editorials also call for a crack-down on crime in the cities and characterize the Negro race as biologically inferior.

A confidential "document" entitled "Zionism: A Documented Outline and Chronology of the Zionist Master Plan for World Dominion," appears in two installments; it covers the years 1896 through 1919 and attempts to expose the nature of the "Marxist-Jewish Conspiracy," employing a format similar to that of the Protocols.

Editor's Response:

"Thanks for the enclosed description from your viewpoint of The Cross and the Flag. You are to be congratulated on your scholarly undertaking."

National Christian News

Address: Box 10924
        St. Petersburg 33, Florida
Monthly; $2.00 per year
Circulation: Not ascertained

Publication Started: 1963
Format: 4-page tabloid Newspaper
Issues Examined: Nos. 2, 3, 4, 5, 6
    (1965) plus 2 earlier issues

    The National Christian News is a religious, right wing newspaper whose most prominent characteristic is its anti-Jewish orientation. Every article excoriates the Jews. This publication attempts to show that the Jews, a hidden government, control the United States, and indeed the world. Jews control America by means of the Federal Reserve System, and therefore, the National Christian News calls for the abolition of that system.

    The editor says that the only way to fight communism is to recognize that the real enemy behind it is the anti-Christ Jew. On the basis of certain Bible passages, he predicts that World War III is inevitable and imminent and emphasizes preparation for it.

    This paper attempts to prove that Christ was not a Jew, the Bible is not Jewish, the Jews are guilty of the murder of Christ, and they were not the chosen people of God.

    National Christian News is also against integration. The Civil Rights Bill is a "vicious, Godless law." This periodical is also against the "anti-Christ" world council of churches, against the United Nations, against Winston Churchill, and against the idea of "universal brotherhood." It is pro-Nazi claiming that the Nazis helped protect the world from the "Jew-Communists."

    The National Christian News claims to be "an honest institution headed by Christian Patriots with the sole aim of helping to preserve our Christian heritage and freedoms by means of bringing documented truth and Holy Bible Scripture enlightenment to the doubting ones." It also says "We admit we are a hate paper!...Because we hate as almighty God and His Beloved Son Jesus Christ hated."

    This newspaper contains articles by various writers, but the editor and writer of the bulk of material is the Reverend Mr. Oren Fenton Potito.

National Chronicle

Address: P.O. Box AC
    Burney, California 96013
Weekly; $5.00 per year
Circulation: 1,280

Publication Started: 1952
Format: 4-page Newspaper
Issues Examined: Dec. 30, 1965;
    Jan. 13, 27, and 30, 1966

    National Chronicle is anti-Communist, anti-Negro, and anti-Jewish; it puts the three on the same level. In one article, the editors state: "Block in every way possible anything that the Jews, Commies, and Niggers can offer, for all of them will be against the U.S. Constitution." Other statements made along this same line of thought include: "Never send a Coon to do a white man's job"; and "FBI agents are Jew-controlled shock troops of integration. Those criminals are working to destroy our white race." President Johnson is referred to as the "Black Hope of America."

    Some other stands that the publication takes are conservative. In a letter, the editor describes the stand as "pro-Constitutional America." It sees the U.N. as "world Communism in all its blood-stained glory," and asks its readers to offer all the opposition that is possible to the U.N." It is quite concerned with the Rhodesian Independence movement and opposes the action that the United States has taken. "Rhodesians have a much better grasp of the world situation than the American citizen." Also in reference to Africa, there is an article entitled "U.S. Government Not the People---gives $750,000 to Zambia to Teach Cannibals How to Overthrow White Christian Governments." In the article entitled "U.S. Government..." it is stated that "the people of the U.S., that is, the Christian population, are powerless to stop this massacre of their fellow believers for the powerful Zionist-Jew-Communist-Nigger Government of their country is so strongly in favor of the U.N., and the other 97% of the residents "can do nothing." Also expressed in the publication is opposition to the Consular Treaty as "designed to allow the Kremlin to spread espionage centers across America." The ratification of the three treaties with Panama is opposed because it "will surrender our right to defend and keep open this... link between our east... and west coast, and allow this area to become a spy center." The Genocide Treaty is rejected because it is "a powder keg and a two-edged sword that can be used as a vicious weapon."

Editor's Response:
    Editor expressed no disapproval.

National Renaissance Bulletin

Address: 10 West 90th Street
        New York, New York 10024
Irregular; $3.00 per 12 issues
Circulation: Not ascertained

Publication Started: 1950
Format: 4- to 12-page Newsletter
Issues Examined: March-April-May, and June-Dec., 1965

National Renaissance Bulletin is the official organ of the National Renaissance Party, a political party whose aim is to establish a strong, centralized Racial Nationalist State including the United States and Canada and limiting citizenship to mentally and genetically sound members of the Caucasian Race.

This publication repeatedly emphasizes that "RACE and not ECONOMICS constitutes the basic key to the cipher of historical understanding and the correct interpretation of major political and social upheavals."

The most prevalent concern of the National Renaissance Bulletin is the Jewish question. This party sees the Jews as being "behind all phases of revolutionary and anti-nationalistic agitation," and holds that "the detrimental effect of alien Hebraic thought upon Western society has resulted in the creation of effeminate, pacifist-minded, and thoroughly graft-ridden systems of government known technically as parliamentary democracies." It also sees the Jew as controlling the financial system of the nation.

The official program of the National Renaissance Party includes purging the Jews from cultural, economic, and political life; returning Negroes to Africa; and subsidizing the birth of healthy, white children.

Its economic program is based on the principle that the interests of the individual are subordinate to those of the nation. The party sees capitalism as not constitutionally based. Specific aspects of the economic program include nationalization of the Federal Reserve and private banking system to take it out of Jewish control; ownership by the state of 50% of the total stocks of major industries; elimination of the struggle between labor and management; an assured minimum income and a maximum limit on income per family; elimination of taxes; death penalty for usury; and elimination of unemployment.

In foreign policy, the National Renaissance Party advocates a United Europe as a bulwark against "the colored hordes of Asia" and a policy of "Africa for the black Africans" and "Asia for the Asiatics."

The National Renaissance Party places a great deal of emphasis on social issues advocating free college education, free hospitalization for the needy, increased aid to the aged (but elimination of social security deductions), sterilization of sexual deviates and mental defectives, and the death penalty for prostitution, sale of narcotics, and distribution of pornographic material.

The National Renaissance Bulletin escoriates Christianity as "a hybrid theological monstrosity"; brotherhood as a product of "absurd mouthings and ranting of crazed Christian zealots"; and the John Birch Society because its members are "concerned more with profits than with ideals of racial preservation."

Editor's Response:
"I will not find fault with the quotations contained therein but would suggest that a study of the enclosed party program might more accurately balance the positive aspects of our world outlook with the negative values..." Changes in the text were made accordingly.

The Pilgrim Torch

Address: P.O. Box 257
         Englewood, Colorado
Bimonthly; $2.00 per year
Circulation: 50,000

Publication Started: 1946
Format: 20-page Magazine
Issues Examined: April-May and June-July, 1965

The Pilgrim Torch, published by the Soldiers of the Cross, presents an anti-Communist, white-supremacist point of view. "Christian patriotism" is advocated.

Articles such as "The Intellectual Dupes of Communism" and "Fidel Castro Red Monster" depict Communism as immoral, atheistic and inhuman. Economics is rarely the issue in The Pilgrim Torch. A series of articles entitled "The Race Problem in the United States," by Americanus, argues for white, Aryan supremacy. The author presents the thesis that there are only two races of man, white and black, and that all other peoples of the earth are a mixture of these two; only the Northern Europeans and their descendants are pure Caucasians.

Articles such as "George Washington: A Man of Two Eras," and "A Living Document" (a commentary of the Declaration of Independence and the men who signed it, published by Life Line) present the "Christian patriotic" point of view.

"From the Desk of the Editor," a collection of news items and short commentaries of topical interest, gives such information as crime rates among Negroes, the formation of the Progressive Labor Party, and the election of Pedro Arrupe as the head of the Jesuit order.

The Rockwell Report

Address: Box 22071
         Dallas, Texas 75222
Monthly; $10 per year
Circulation: 8,000

Publication Started: 1961
Format: 16-page Newsletter
Issues Examined: March 1965

The Rockwell Report, a publication of the American Nazi Party, includes feature articles by George Lincoln Rockwell. In the lead article of the March 1965 issue entitled "Rockwell for Governor - the Virginia Campaign Opens," Rockwell states that "there is no longer any doubt that we can win political power in the state of Virginia." He discusses the political climate in Virginia, telling Nazi Party members what they could do to help get his name on the ballot. The issue also contains a very caustic review of the one-act plays The Toilet and The Slave, written by Negro playwright LeRoi Jones. It also discusses "Military Degeneracy," "The Golden Ghetto" (a description of the Jewish people in Miami Beach), and "Lest We Forget the Nature of the Blacks."

The Stormtrooper

Address: P. O. Box 22071
        Dallas, Texas 75222
Quarterly; $1.00 per year
Circulation: 55,000

Publication Started: 1962 (superseding National Socialist Bulletin)
Format: Small size Magazine with about 48-pages
Issues Examined: Winter 1965

The Stormtrooper is the "official news magazine of the American Nazi Party" and contains the editorial comments of the party commander, George Lincoln Rockwell, as well as numerous articles by other party members. Photographs, cartoons, and quotations from other sources are also used extensively. The Stormtrooper includes regular features entitled "Combat Reports," "Bits of Bigotry," "International Nazi News," and "Know Your Officers," as well as sections devoted to letters to the editor and sales listings of Nazi literature and other items.

The Winter 1965 issue contains articles entitled "The Coming Race War," "Nazi in Blackface Invades Congress," "California Battlefront," and "Little Known Facts about Adolf Hitler." This issue also includes a section entitled "International Nazi Progress," which reports on Nazi progress in England, the United States, Italy, Iceland, France, Germany, Chile, Holland, Canada, and South Africa.

The Thunderbolt

Address: P. O. Box 184
        Augusta, Georgia
Monthly; (presently irregular) $3.00 per year
Circulation: 25,000

Publication Started: 1963 (?)
Format: 12-page Tabloid Newspaper
Issues Examined: May 1965 and January 1966

The Thunderbolt is the "official White Racial organ of the National States Rights Party" (NSRP). The Thunderbolt presents the viewpoint that a white, Christian America is threatened by Jewish attempts to destroy the white race through the promotion of intermarriage with "black savages." This idea is developed in a lead article, "Jew Kaplan New Head of NAACP." The specific themes of Negro inferiority, "race-mixing" and Jewish-Communist subversion are also discussed in The Thunderbolt, e.g., "Famed Professor Says Average Negro Incapable of 8th Grade Work," "Arrest Exposes Johnny Cash's Negro Wife," and "Communist Jew Leads Illegal Delegation to North Vietnam." The NSRP also advocates the deportation of all Negroes to Africa. The party participates in the political process in the hopes of gaining the power needed to "solve America's problems."

Editor's Response:
    The summary is fair and correct.

Truth Seeker

Address: P.O. Box 2832
     San Diego, California
Monthly; $3.00 per year
Circulation: 1,400

Publication Started: 1873
Format: 16-page Magazine
Issues Examined: July, August, and September 1965

The Truth Seeker, which describes itself as the "oldest freethought paper in the world," includes articles expressing an atheistic white-supremacist point of view. Writers express the belief that they are being deprived of their basic liberties by "masses of whites degenerated by the destructive venom of Christianity and the cunning propaganda of certain organized Jews, their Communist allies, and the blackskin revolutionaries."

Marshall J. Gauvin asks, "Is There a Single Sound Reason for believing in God?" and discusses the contradictions between the existence of "a wise and good God" and the present world situation. "The Catholic Church, the World's Greatest Capitalist" expresses sharp criticism of the Church's tax exemptions.

Each issue of Truth Seeker contains lists of recommended pamphlets and books dealing largely with religious criticism and race theories.

Editor's Response:

"The Truth Seeker tells objective truth, whether it is heretical or not; we are not actually a white supremacist paper as your review states, but we do champion the white race, now under so heavy an attack by the Leftists. We are almost the only periodical in the U.S. which tells the truth on all matters. Most others are afraid of religionists, the Catholic Church, the Jews, the Negroes, the medical monopoly, or other powerful interests. Our appeal is to intellectuals, objective thinkers, particularly those who want to see human happiness increased."

The White American

Address: P.O. Box 8399
     Ensley Station
     Birmingham, Alabama
Monthly (irregular): except December; $3.00 per year
Circulation: Not ascertained

Publication Started: Not ascertained
Format: 16-page Magazine
Issues Examined: March, April-May, Sept.-Oct., 1965; June, 1966

The White American is the official publication of the National White Americans Party (formerly the American States Rights Party), a splinter group from the National States Rights Party. Its purpose is "to inform, educate, and bring unity to the 150,000,000 white Americans in our republic... it is our expressed purpose to reclaim the United States of America for the white race which gave it birth."

The White American is "against the Negro race and for that matter any inferior colored race, being citizens of the United States," and it urges "repatriation of the black race to Africa." A major purpose of the magazine is to convey "to the general public scientific, genetic, social, economic, and cultural reasons" for this repatriation.

The White American contains such reports as that of a group of Negroes picketing a white brothel, of cannibalism among Negroes in Africa and America, and of open lovemaking during the Selma march. It is strongly anti-Jewish and anti-Communist, reporting on the "Jewish-Communist conspiracy" behind the Los Angeles race riots. It opposes the United Nations, calling it the greatest single instrument of Communist power. It is against the National Council of Churches, declaring that "the National Council of Churches and Jews unite to destroy the white race." It opposes the present Administration of the U.S., which is creating the greatest threat by "scrapping our current immigration system and admitting the garbage of inferior races."

The White American contains various other items, such as a plea for a word from a missing teenager; Patrick Henry's famous speech; a "Letter from a Young Communist"; a memorial to Matt Murphy, who defended Collie Leroy Wilkins in court; the platform of the National White Americans Party; some verse concerning the odor of Negroes; and reviews of television programs featuring Negro cowboys.

Among the many illustrations in this publication are items such as copy of advertisements for hair straightener and skin bleach from Negro magazines, and drawings showing the resemblance of Negroes to apes.

Editor's Response:
"The summary does represent a true and accurate account of articles and features published in the White American."

Chapter 6
RIGHT OF CENTER

American Flag Committee Newsletter

Address: 2834 Almond Street
Philadelphia, Pennsylvania
19134
Published as the occasion demands:
$4.00 for 12 issues
Circulation: 5,000

Publication Started: August 10, 1950
Format: 4-page Newsletter,
mimeographed
Issues Examined: Spring, Summer,
and September, 1965

The American Flag Committee Newsletter, the official organ of the American Flag Committee, reveals the organization's concern about Communist infiltration and take over of the civil rights movement and Communist exploitation of Negro discontent. For example, the newsletter alleges that the civil rights activities of the last few years, centering around voting rights, have been masterminded by the Communist Party, through its "Lincoln Project," formulated in 1956. It further claims that the 1965 Voting Rights Act and the Selma-Montgomery march were planned in accordance with the aims of this project, which were to force Federal legislation through direct action. The American Flag Committee also claims that one of the major causes of the Los Angeles riots was a public hearing held by California Negro Congressman Augustus F. Hawkins concerning the administration of the anti-poverty program in Los Angeles County. It was said that the Federal government was trying to subvert local government through the anti-poverty funds into private civil rights and radical labor groups. The committee also claims that this alleged subversion and Federal centralization are Communist goals.

Editor's Response:
"Although in recent issues we have devoted much coverage to what we consider to be Communist domination of the civil rights movement, we have published much material in opposition to the accretion of Federal power in other areas, to the United Nations and NATO as potential structures for the elaboration of World Government, and to the imposition of so-called 'mental health' laws which compromise basic constitutional rights, such as trial by jury, habeas corpus, and elimination of the accepted rules of evidence and the right to enter a plea."

The American Mercury

Address: P. O. Box 1306
Torrance, Cal. 90505
Quarterly: $10.00 per year (includes semi-monthly Washington Observer Newsletter.)
Circulation: 10,000

Publication Started: 1924
Format: Small size, 52- to 60-page Magazine
Issues Examined: Sept. and Autumn 1965; Feb. and June 1966

The American Mercury is a conservative publication. It opposes Communism and internationalism and sees internationalism as part of the world revolution of Communism. Articles deal with topics of current interest in an editorial fashion. For example in the September 1965 issue Edwin A. Walker states that the "U. N., NATO, OAS, SEATO, the Vatican, NCC, AFL-CIO, the Supreme Court, and the International Bank" are "an unseen international world government performing its purpose of 'Global Conquest.'"

In the Autumn 1965 issue it is stated: "The U. N. is only the front for the real power that operates as a sovereign entity behind the scenes. The international group dictates to this and that power, including the U. N." In the same issue, Clymer Wright, Jr. expresses the belief that our defense program is inadequate for the future. The February 1966 issue contains an article by W. A. Carto in which he calls for the Conservatives to use more political action to win elections. Another article quotes from the Shreveport Times as follows: "The Washington idea seems to be to do a lot of air bombing, but to make sure that North Vietnam is not really hurt... take the handcuffs [sic] and the Air Force could wipe North Vietnam off the map." Judge John R. Rarick calls for a "reapportionment of voting procedures in the United Nations because he believes that as it now stands, the smaller nations have more power than they deserve; and Dean Lindy states that the New Left is an "anti-intellectual" movement. The June 1966 issue contains an article debating the need of a new political party in the United States. Bert Ellis says that we do need a new party which would be the Constitution Party. Bruce Evans opposes this stating that the new party needed should be within the already existing Republican Party.

Reference is not infrequently made to the Bible. An anti-Jewish orientation is also perceived, as may be seen in this quote from an article attempting to disprove the "six million" figure of Jews killed in Germany: "No scientifically valid proofs were ever adduced for the fantastic charge of six million, repeated and elaborated ad nauseum."

Subscribers to The American Mercury receive, at no extra cost, the Washington Observer Newsletter, which is published semi-monthly except February 1, June 1, September 1, and December 1, the issue dates for The American Mercury.

Washington Observer Newsletter, a 4-page newsletter, is similar in orientation to that of The American Mercury. The July 1 edition, for example, carries an article on Defense Secretary McNamara that contends, "The ill-considered Act of 1958 paved the way for the advent of a Caesar in our republic, and, sure enough, in 1961 we got McNamara... Among other things, McCaesar is a graduate of Berkeley California, University--hot-bed of subversion."

Editor's Response:
(The following is from the American Mercury Style Sheet, June 1966) "Reorganization of MERCURY has as its aim the gradual reestablishment of the magazine as a lively, thought-provoking family journal covering many different facets of life in America and Western Civilization, and grounded in the best of the tradition of the West. Chief requirement of articles is that they be widely interesting and of a basically constructive nature."

American Opinion

Address: 395 Concord Avenue
Belmont, Massachusetts
02178
Monthly (except July); $10 per year
Circulation: 47,000

Publication Started: 1958
Format: Small size, 112-page Magazine
Issues Examined: January, February, and March 1965

American Opinion, a monthly magazine, presents conservative opinions on political, economic, and social questions as well as the arts. The magazine "uses almost no articles except those written to order to fit (their) specific needs." Two related problems seem to reflect the overriding concern of the magazine's editors: problems caused by the "International Communist Conspiracy" abroad and by "Liberals" or "Socialists" at home.

Harold Lord Varney's article about recent events in Panama states that the United States has been unable to deal effectively with the problems of revolution abroad because its leaders have been hesitant to use American power. Instead of making an open display of our power, compelling the Communists to retreat, we have succumbed to the demands of miniscule countries and to far-left political influence at home, he maintains.

The magazine also focuses on Communist activity in domestic affairs, such as Communist infiltration of the peace and civil rights movements. Citing reports of the House Un-American Activities Committee, James J. Drummey discusses various peace groups and remarks that their members are Communists, Communist sympathizers, or tools of the "International Communist Conspiracy."

American Opinion also criticizes "Liberal" or "Socialist" ideas and activities related to domestic affairs. Martin Dies contends that "Liberal" policies will inevitably lead to "Socialism", an economic system which requires a political dictatorship. In this manner, the most fundamental freedoms are being placed in jeopardy by "Liberals," he adds. Professor Hans Sennholz notes that the type of "giveaway" programs initiated to cure health, education, housing, and unemployment problems break down the moral fiber of our people, and he criticizes "The Great Society." American Opinion attacks the Liberal assumption that "there is no sin but only unfortunate circumstances" as helping to produce immorality and crime. In "For Morality," Jim Lucier deplores the breakdown of traditional morality and expresses the conviction that the individual is responsible for making decisions based upon moral standards which are not relative, but absolute. Other articles blame a large bureaucratic society for the breakdown of individual moral responsibility.

The editor, Robert Welch, states that American Opinion is not the organ of the John Birch Society and less than half of its subscribers are members of the John Birch Society.

Editor's Response:
"Even though our articles are mostly written to order, and to fit our specific needs in the sense that we want them on subjects in which we are most interested, and written basically from the Conservative viewpoint, you have to realize just how much Conservative individualists in America disagree with each other on practically everything, in order to understand the divergence of opinion and even conclusions which thus shows up in our pages. And we give all of our writers, but especially those who seem to be most controversial, a great deal of leeway in this respect."

"For example, nearly three years ago there was an article written to order for us -- at the request of our Managing Editor, incidentally, and not of myself (Robert Welch) -- by Dr. Revilo Oliver, dealing with the assassination of President Kennedy. Some of the opinions and conclusions expressed in that article were so contrary to my own that, on reading the article in page proofs, I took the opportunity of stating in the 'Letter to the Reader' on the inside front cover of that very issue, and then later stated more emphatically and more at length in other places, that there was this decided disagreement with regard to several passages in Dr. Oliver's article."

America's Future

Address: 542 Main Street
         New Rochelle, New York
Weekly; $5.00 per year
Circulation: 6,500

Publication Started: 1959
Format: Small size, 8-page Magazine
Issues Examined: July 23, August 27, and September 17, 1965

America's Future, a "weekly review of news, books and public affairs," supports a belief in the "God-given freedom of the individual, a belief in the Constitution of the United States as it was originally written, and a belief in the capitalist free enterprise economic system." America's Future, Inc., states that it is the "combination of a free economic system and a constitutional republic that has made the United States unique as the freest and most abundant nation on the earth." It adds that the greatest threats to this system are "atheistic Communism, its knowing and unknowing Socialist allies, and Big Government in general."

America's Future summarizes items covered in the America's Future, Inc., Mutual Network radio broadcasts; reprints articles from other sources; and reviews a book in each weekly issue. For example, the July 23, 1965, issue summarizes a broadcast describing the work of the Textbook Evaluation Committee set up by America's Future, Inc. An article entitled "Real Censors" discusses the criticism the National Education Association had made of this committee. The Textbook Evaluation Committee stated that the NEA acted as the real censor of books by seeking to smear those disagreeing with their point of view.

The August 27, 1965 issue of America's Future discusses the Los Angeles riots, stating that no socio-economic reasons could be presented as excuses for rioting, anarchy, and lack of respect for the law. The policies of several Negro leaders, specifically, Martin Luther King, also receive criticism. The book The Sheepskin Psychosis is reviewed in this issue.

The September 17, 1965 issue features articles entitled "Dominican Backdown," "Labor Union-Political Monopoly," "Union Slaves," and a book review of The Great Boom and Panic by Robert Patterson.

Editor's Response:
"We have no objections to the proposed piece."

The Capital Voice

Address: 1501 Farragut Street S.W.
         Washington, D.C. 20011
Monthly; $2.00 per year
Circulation: 30,000

Publication Started: 1952
Format: 8-page Newsletter
Issues Examined: Dec. 1, 1965, Jan. 1 and Feb. 1, 1966

The Capital Voice is a religious publication which touches on political issues but does not go into them in depth. Each of the articles even concerning politics has a religious moral. The editor, Evangelist Dale Crowley, writes the majority of the articles. With regard to the war in Vietnam, he says that "we are fighting an undeclared war, which is unconstitutional" and that "Congress should face up to its responsibility in this matter" by declaring war. "We tried this program of fighting an undeclared war in Korea, and it didn't work... Why do we think it will work differently in Vietnam?" He has no faith in the United Nations as an answer to the world's problems: "The U.N. does not have the power or the courage or the character to silence the blatant blasphemous voice of red, atheistic Communism in its sessions; but instead... has allowed itself to become the sounding board for Soviet propaganda." He is against internationalism: "The wolves of internationalism are closing in on us. These one-worlders and Communist sympathizers are out to destroy us." And he is not in favor of the Johnson administration: "... no member of the Great Society must have anything to worry about. The only condition is that they must not think."

Each issue contains an editorial column, "Thinking Out Loud," in which various topics are discussed. In December, Mr. Crowley stated that it was the duty of Secretary McNamara to see that the "deplorable practice of making liquor available to our enlisted men" be stopped. In January, concerning the war in Vietnam, it is to be the decision of Congress, not just a resolution of the president. The February editorial dealt with President Johnson's State of the Union message and the defects of the Great Society. Also in each issue, are excerpts from a radio message by Mr. Crowley which takes the form of a sermon.

Besides the articles of pure religious orientation, there are those speaking out against drinking and smoking and short articles on pornography, the "new morality," and crime.

Editor's Response:
"On the whole the characterizations are well stated."

Christian Anti-Communism Crusade

Address: P.O. Box 890
124 East First Street
Long Beach, California
90801
Published irregularly, at least once a month; contributions solicited
Circulation: 50,000

Publication Started: 1961
Format: 8-page Newsletter
Issues Examined: August and September 1965; March 21 and April 4, 1966

The Christian Anti-Communism Crusade's newsletter appears as an open letter, on two or three topics, to the members and non-members of the Crusade from the Crusade's President, Dr. Fred Schwarz. There may be articles by other writers, as well as a section which gives information about films, tapes, records and books with an anti-Communist theme, which are available to the public. News of the Crusade's projects, such as a four-day anti-Communist school, and of fund-raising drives needing support is also given.

In the August 1965 newsletter, Dr. Schwarz discusses, "Reds, Race, Riots, and Revolution." He begins his letter with a quotation from the Peking Review: "At all times and in all circumstance Marxist-Leninists are promoters of revolution." Dr. Schwarz states that it is imperative for Crusade members to understand the Communists' revolutionary tactics and emphasizes that the Communists will always attempt to use the grievances of the Negro, both "legitimate and illegitimate" for their own subversive purposes. Dr. Schwarz also takes the opportunity in this newsletter to condemn Negroes' alleged hatred of symbols of authority, particularly the police. He defends the police in his letter as well as in a special message entitled "Thank God for the Police."

Among other articles in the issues examined there was one discussing the possible existence of offensive missiles in Cuba, and another concerning the susceptibility of the "New Left" (student radicals) and the "Old Left" (disillusioned Communists) to today's Communist Party.

Editor's Response:
"The newsletter attempts a review of current Communist strategy and tactics as revealed in such Communist literature as the 'Peking Review', the 'World Marxist Review', 'Political Review' and the 'Worker'. Documentation from these sources is copious." (Note: the Editor probably meant "Political Affairs," not "Political Review.")

CHRISTIAN BEACON

Address: 756 Haddon Avenue
Collingswood, New Jersey
Weekly; $2.00 per year
Circulation: Not ascertained

Publication Started: 1936
Format: 8- to 16- page tabloid Newspaper
Issues Examined: 8 issues between June 24 and September 9, 1965

The Christian Beacon, edited by Carl McIntire, is a weekly newspaper. The nonprofit corporation that sponsors the 20th Century Reformation Hour, a weekly radio program, is its sponsor. Both the newspaper and the radio program represent the views of the Bible Presbyterian Church, (a fundamentalist Presbyterian group which broke away from the United Presbyterian Church, USA,) and the National and International Councils of Christian Churches, fundamentalist counterparts to the National and World Councils of Churches.

According to Jon Reid Kennedy, who often writes for the Christian Beacon, a fundamentalist is one who maintains "strict adherence to the doctrines of verbal inspiration of the scriptures, the virgin birth of Christ, His absolute and essential deity, His bodily resurrection, and His Second Coming..." Christian Beacon fundamentalists distinguish themselves from "evangelicals," whom they consider too prone to compromise, as well as from the bodies of Christians represented by the World Council of Churches and the Roman Catholic Church.

The Christian Beacon presents rightist political views. Quite often it accuses the churches outside the National and International Council of Christian Churches of cooperating with and sanctioning Communism. In the issues reviewed, the U.N., political liberalism, as well as socialism and Communism, and the proposal to repeal Section 14b of the Taft-Hartley Act (which allows states to forbid the union shop) are specifically attacked. In an article "Is Christianity Political?" by Kenneth Myers, Lt. Col. USAF, it is stated that "Jesus refused point-blank to be a socialist equalizer between men. He was never a welfare stater. Thus...Jesus was not a collectivist, nor a socialist or statist, but an individualist."

The actual coverage of the Christian Beacon centers around the activities of the organizations whose views it represents; articles discuss accreditation of their college, Shelton College, various tours, rallies, services and meetings. A regular feature is the "Weekly Bible School Lesson."

CHRISTIAN CRUSADE

Address: 2808 South Sheridan Road
Tulsa, Oklahoma 74102
Monthly; $2.00 per year
Circulation: 87,000

Publication Started: 1948
Format: 32-page Magazine
Issues Examined: May, June, July 1959; July, December 1965, and January 1966

Christian Crusade is the monthly magazine of the organization of the same name headed by Dr. Billy James Hargis, a "lay organization... based on Christian principles... (which aims) to effectively meet the challenge of Communism."

The magazine consists largely of reports and discussions of the various activities of the organization, including the Christian Crusade Anti-Communist Youth University at Manitou Springs, Colorado. The "University" holds seminars during the summer for "Christian conservative children, fourteen years and older" to teach them "the unvarnished truth regarding Communism, Socialism, and their traceable offsprings in the fields of religion, economics, politics, education and culture."

Mildred Clarke, the National Membership Correspondent of the Christian Crusade, gives chapter news and encourages members to set up new chapters, stating that this would be "the most important anti-Communist work anyone can do."

"Crusader's Journal" by Hargis covers tours, conventions and fund-raising drives. In "Holy Land Tour is a Mountain-Top Experience," Hargis discusses the latest tour sponsored by the Christian Crusade - that of Europe and the Middle East - and presents his interviews with Generalissimo Franco of Spain and Senator Barry Goldwater. He also discusses the fund raising for the construction of the building which will house the Crusade's cathedral, headquarters, and training center.

On the question of the possible removal of the tax-exempt status of the Christian Crusade, David Noebel states that he cannot understand the reasons behind the Internal Revenue Service's threat to the Christian Crusade regarding the removal of its tax-exempt status when religious organizations with headquarters in Washington - such as the National Catholic Welfare Conference - are engaged in political lobbying and are retaining their tax-exempt status. Dr. W. O. H. Garman, in his article attacking the National Council of Churches, states that this is simply discrimination.

Christian Crusade gives prime attention to the problem of Communism and revolutionary movements. Dr. Fernando Penabez discusses the alleged brutal and inhuman activities of Angolan insurgents, remarking that the terrorists in Angola are agents of Marxists like Holden Roberto and Patrice Lumumba. In a book review of The Fearful Master by G. Edward Griffin it is stated that, for the most part, the men involved in the formulation of the U.N. Charter "were men possessed with the obsession of making the world safe for communism."

Editor's Response:
The Editor suggested some minor corrections that have been incorporated in the text.

Christian Economics

Address: 250 West 57th Street
    New York 19, New York
Twice weekly; free on request but
    contributions are solicited
Circulation: 200,000

Publication Started: 1948
Format: 4-page tabloid Newspaper
Issues Examined: April 6, 20,
    May 4, 18, June 1, 15, and 19, 1965

Christian Economics devotes itself to "a discussion of the fundamental problems of economics, especially as related to Christianity and freedom." Foreign affairs and domestic issues that are not specifically economic are also discussed however. Each issue features "Voice of the Editor," a column of editorials; a "Sermonette" written by a different minister or layman in each issue; "The Bible and Economics," written by Rev. T. E. Howard; a book review section; and Letters to the Editor.

The primary concerns of Christian Economics seem to be (1) the question of socialism and the welfare state system versus laissez-faire on the economic front; (2) the decline of morality and loss of religious belief and attitudes in the United States; (3) the problem of Communist attempts at world domination abroad.

Vigorously opposed to socialism or the welfare state system, in an editorial, "The Cause and Cure of Fiscal Problems," Christian Economics advocates a return to the free market. In a free market, prices and wages would be determined by what consumers are willing to pay and each worker would be rewarded in proportion to his contribution. Total output would increase as a result of greater individual incentive - the incentive of knowing that one would be permitted to enjoy the full fruits of his efforts. When the State uses dictatorial authority to achieve a planned economy, it suppresses freedom and incentive, which in turn results in a lower production and standard of living, the editors note.

Howard W. Kacy's "America at the Crossroads" indicates that America is suffering from a serious decay in morality, including massive law-breaking on the part of youngsters, such as rioting, Fair-Play-for-Cuba demonstrations and other serious offenses against the moral order. He suggests that the causes for such lawlessness include a deprecation of discipline stemming from belief in the theory that crime is a product of environmental conditions, courts which protect the criminal at the expense of the victim, corruption in political circles, a deprecation of the law resulting from tactics in the civil rights arena, and a movement to eliminate religion from all aspects of national life.

In "Where is the Kingdom?" Rev. Harry Butman points out that the false hopes of Socialists, who wish to establish a "heaven on earth," are indeed misleading. It is this sort of reasoning that is causing us to lose sight of the spiritual values of Christianity and the essential spiritual nature of man, he remarks. Rev. Butman expresses the view that Jesus had no political mission and rejects the attempts of some clergymen to try to bring the church into line with the world.

Editor's Response:
"In general, I would say it is fair and satisfactory though quite inadequate to reflect the full scope of Christian Economics. In general, and in reference to the second paragraph of what you have written, we do not advocate laissez-faire. There is an important place for government. Government must conduct foreign affairs, provide for the common defense, restrain and punish predation, provide laws governing such matters as inheritance, public health... traffic regulations and many other matters. It is difficult to define accurately the proper zone for the

exercise of governmental power and the proper zone for individual initiative.... I am certain, however, that the zone occupied by government has been unduly enlarged and should be restricted in favor of expanding the zone reserved for the exercise of free initiative.

Specifically, what you have said about the articles of the Reverend Mr. Butman and Mr. Kacy is satisfactory."

The Dan Smoot Report

Address: P.O. Box 9538
    Lakewood Station
    Dallas, Texas 75214
Weekly; $10 per year
Circulation: 40,000

Publication Started: 1955
Format: 4-page Newsletter
Issues Examined: Several 1963 issues, March 22, 29, April 5, 12, and Oct. 25, 1965

In his Report, Dan Smoot notes that he attempts to "use fundamental American constitutional principles as the yardstick for measuring the political and social and economic problems of out time." Quite often he charges that the Federal Government no longer follows the principles of the Constitution, for the Constitution does not provide for the exercise of Federal authority in many of the areas in which the Federal Government is now active. The passage of the Drug Industry Law of 1962, which provides for controls over the manufacture and sale of drugs, is exemplary of illegitimate Congressional action, according to Smoot; he maintains that the Federal Government might take advantage of its newly-acquired powers to administer drugs to an unwitting population and thus perpetuate its control over the public; he fears that Federal control will hurt the drug industry. Smoot also cautions the Federal Government to stay completely out of the areas of housing and urban renewal and to respect the rights of private property and of the individual states.

The Dan Smoot Report also contends that the defense and foreign policies of America's postwar administrations have been unconstitutional. Only by an unwarranted stretch of meaning can the words "national defense" be taken to mean that America's own defense depends upon her protecting the so-called "free world," he asserts. Thus, all foreign aid, both economic and military, should be terminated and the defense budget radically cut, according to Smoot.

Smoot advocates abolishing the income tax structure and thus releasing about two-thirds of the tax money which the Federal Government takes from individuals and corporations for private use. He maintains that such a move would result in greater economic growth and a reduction in unemployment.

In the October 25, 1965 issue of his Report, Mr. Smoot discusses education. After quoting the U.S. Office of Education, which states that "education is a primary instrument for social advancement and human welfare," Smoot asks, "What happened to knowledge, scholarship, discipline, intelligence?" He states that John Dewey, influential educator of the early 20th century, was one of those intellectuals who "readily responded to the tired, cynical, and sickly socialist philosophy imported from Europe." He condemns the National Education Association and National Student Association for their left-wing orientation and "Socialist-Communist doctrines."

Mr. Smoot calls the civil rights movement "a Communist creation intended to foment racial civil war." He states: "The non-Communist agency which has done the most to precipitate civil turmoil is the Supreme Court of the United States under Chief Justice Earl Warren." The four Issues, March 22, March 29, April 5, and April 12, are discussions of the "Earl Warren Court," ending with a plea for the impeachment of Chief Justice Warren.

Editor's Response:
Except for one paragraph, the editor felt that the commentary was reasonably correct. The paragraph in question was deleted.

The Dart Bulletin

Address: P.O. Box 805
    Red Bank, New Jersey
Twice Monthly
Circulation: Not ascertained

Publication Started: 1962
Format: 4-page mimeographed Newsletter
Issues Examined: Sept. 13, and Nov. 22, 1965; Jan. 15, 1966

The Dart Bulletin is a newsletter from Paul Dickson. Contained within it are articles covering a variety of world and national topics, written in an editorial manner. Mr. Dickson feels that changes should be made in the U.S. foreign policy. "Our Washington strategists fire in all directions---against the American people. Sometimes it is indeed hard to know which side they are and for whom they are fighting." He favors the war in Vietnam but doesn't think that our policy there is strong enough: "Washington is shooting the Communists...but...is doing it in a nice way." He is against the oil embargo placed on Rhodesia because the government of the country is now non-Communist and by placing this embargo he feels the U.S. is aiding the pro-Communist forces. Also, he writes unfavorably about our policy in India, which he describes as a "nation who double-crossed the U.S. many times, and violated international laws and the U.N. charter with an act of cowardly armed aggression" against Portugese Goa and Pakistan.

One article approved Albert Schweitzer's views on the U.N. policy in Africa, which had caused him great anxiety because it proceeded from a total ignorance of the country's problems. "If Katanga is unwilling to be returned with the Congo, the U.N. should respect its wishes..." An article praising Dr. Salazar stated that "his foreign policy is an example of uprightness amidst the international spectacle of chicanery and lack of integrity." An article concerned with the strike of the Transport Workers

Union in New York City condemned the workers for striking and praised Mayor Lindsey's handling of the issue.

Editor's Response:
"My opinions are not subordinated to any political party, creed or government. On what concerns the United States, I will fight against anything that in my judgement may constitute a menace to our Democracy or may be detrimental to America's integrity and prestige abroad and at home."
 The Editor further stated that he found the summary accurate, clear, and to the point.

Economic Council Letter

Address: Suite 1100
          156 Fifth Avenue
          New York, New York 10010
Semimonthly (except monthly during the summer); $10.00 per year
Circulation: Not ascertained

Publication Started: 1930
Format: 4-page Newsletter
Issues Examined: June 15, 1965; July 1965; August 1965; May 1, 1966 June 15, 1966; June 1, 1966

The Economic Council Letter is published semimonthly by the National Economic Council, Inc., a "nonprofit, nonpartisan membership corporation." The Economic Council strives "to prevent increases in government spending, to arouse opposition to unilateral disarmament, to unbuild the Federal bureaucracy, to subtract the privileged position from unresponsible labor, to retain the Connally Reservation, and to reduce inflationary pressures."
 Each issue of the newsletter is devoted to the discussion of one or more topics. The May 1, 1966 issue, "All Too Quiet On the Potomac," discusses the lack of resistance to government power and spending. The May 15 issue, "Why Are We Still Losing?" includes a discussion of the added value tax. The June 1 Letter is entitled "The Frustrated Middle Classes."

Editor's Response:
 Editor expressed no disapproval.

The Fact Finder

Address: Box 10555
          Phoenix, Arizona 85016
Biweekly; $5 for 2 subscriptions
Circulation: Not ascertained

Publication Started: 1942
Format: 8-page Pamphlet
Issues Examined: June 30, October 31, 1965

The Fact Finder defends a constitutional, representative form of government and the free enterprise system, attacking Communist and Socialist subversion within the United States and Communist plans for world domination. The Fact Finder especially warns about supposed Communist activity within the Federal Government and the public apathy concerning this activity. These views are expressed in issues entitled, for example, "What the President May Not know about the Revolution" and "The Communists Can Take Over the World without a Big War."

Editor's Response:
"OK as corrected." (Suggested corrections have been incorporated into the text.)

Firing Line

Address: P.O. Box 1055
 Indianapolis, Indiana
 46206
Monthly; $3.00 per year
Circulation: Not ascertained

Publication Started: 1952
Format: 8-page Newsletter
Issues Examined: July and other issues in 1965

Firing Line is published by the American Legion's National Americanism Commission. This eight-page report discusses the activities of Communist and Communist-front organizations and offers advice to readers on how to counteract the work of subversive groups. One issue reviewed contained a lead article entitled "Commanding Thoughts," as well as a series of shorter articles and miscellany, including the results of polls, summaries of Supreme Court decisions, reprints from other publications, etc. Photographs and cartoons are also used in the publication.

The July 1965 issue concentrates on the question of Communists speaking on college campuses. The lead article, "Communist Campaign against the U.S.," discusses speeches given on campuses by Gus Hall, the General Secretary of the Communist Party, U.S.A. The results of a poll sponsored by the National Americanism Commission concerning Communist speakers on campuses are printed in this issue, along with summaries of four recent Supreme Court decisions related to Communist activity in the United States. The issue also contains an article on Communist influences in the civil rights movement and a special reprint, "The U.S. Businessman Faces the Soviet Spy," by J. Edgar Hoover.

Freedom's Facts

Address: 1028 Connecticut Avenue,
 N.W.
 Washington, D.C. 20036
Monthly; $3.00 per year
Circulation: 3,000

Publication Started: 1950
Format: 4-page Newsletter
Issues Examined: February, June, August, 1965

Freedom's Facts is a publication of the All-American Conference to Combat Communism, an organization "which includes some 40 national veterans, women's fraternal, civil, religious and youth organizations," among which are the American Legion Auxiliary, Lions International, and the Elks. "Its purpose is to provide organization leaders and others with accurate information on the aims, programs and techniques of Communists and others who seek to destroy the free principles and institutions which these organizations support."

Freedom's Facts analyzes Communist-leftist activity both at home and abroad and reports on world events that relate to Communist activity. Titles of articles include "Marxists Open New Classes for Students and Youth," "Singapore-Malaysia Break," and "Guerilla Warfare: Can We Win It?". Features include "International Dateline," "World Trade Notes," and "World Scope."

Editor's Response:
"The summary of Freedom's Facts is quite good."

Freedom's Way

Address: P.O. Box 2173
         Newport Beach, California
         92660
Monthly; $2.00 per year
Circulation: 164 paid

Publication Started: 1964
Format: 4-to 6-page mimeographed Newsletter
Issues Examined: March and April 1966

Freedom's Way describes itself as being "dedicated to the 'Victory' of freedom, reason, and objective principle." Concerning collectivism, W.H. Carroll, the editor, says, "Whether we like it or not--and of course we don't like it--collectivism is the ruling creed...it is steadily gaining material and political strength even as it becomes more obviously bankrupt intellectually." Of three alternatives to fight collectivism, he advocates working "within the existing framework of government and society...in order to change the collectivist course in government and society before it has become irreversible."

The March issue is an article describing the break up of the conservative coalition after the Goldwater defeat. He sees the problem facing the conservatives in 1966 as "whether any comparable coalition can be formed around any other major political figure who shows at least some real promise of moving in the direction of freedom." He believes that in the Congressional elections in 1966, if the Republicans expect to make any substantial gains, the issue should not be the Vietnam War, but "the inflation issue." In addition, he opposes President Johnson's proposed amendment to give Congressmen a four-year term, and calls it "one of the final institutional steps toward unlimited executive power since it would remove even the possibility that voters could apply a check on the President through off-year Congressional elections..."

The publication voices the objectivist philosophy of economics and politics. Mr. Carroll advocates that Ayn Rand's maxim of "check your premises" be applied to the "manner of human persuasion."

Free Enterprise

Address: Box 10555
    Phoenix, Arizona 85016
Monthly; $3.00 per year
Circulation: Not ascertained

Publication Started: Not ascertained
Format: 4- to 8-page tabloid Newspaper
Issues Examined: April, March, October 1965

    Free Enterprise, presenting "action news for anti-Communists," represents the views of the organization, We, the People!" This tabloid covers a variety of anti-Communist and anti-Socialist activities, especially as they relate to governmental affairs. For example, "Reds Gain with Our Gold," the lead article of the April 1965 issue, discusses the findings of the Senate Internal Security Subcommittee concerning Harry Dexter White's alleged sabotage of United States aid to Chiang Kai-shek during the latter's post-war struggle with Mao Tse-tung for the control of mainland China. Another lead article proclaims that on the domestic scene "Socialists Use Democrats to Soften U.S. Resistance to Communism." "Straight Talk," a column written by Tom Anderson, and "Prose and Kahn's," a collection of short, satirical thrusts, as well as several editorials per issue, are regular features of Free Enterprise.

Editor's Response:
    "OK"

The Freeman

Address: Foundation for Economic
    Education, Inc.
    Irvington-on-Hudson, New
    York 10533
Monthly; Financed through voluntary contributions
Circulation: 12,000 contributors; monthly printing of 60,000 as of July, 1965

Publication Started: 1950
Format: Small size, 64-page Magazine
Issues Examined: January, February, March 1965

    The Freeman, which describes itself as "a monthly journal of ideas on liberty," champions the free market economy and limited government. Articles attempt to explain the workings and advantages of a laissez-faire economy. They also attempt to point out the errors in socialistic economic theory and the mistakes of "collectivist" practices. For example, Hans Sennholz and Leonard E. Read explain the classical theory of the relation of prices and demand-value (as opposed to labor-value) and discuss the natural order inherent in the free market economy, an order that any governmental attempts at economic regulation will destroy. "Let's Not Save the World" applies the concept of natural law and laissez-faire policy to political and social problems. "Is God a Keynesian?" and "Let's First Mend Tommy's Trousers" advocate self-help and the economic and social freedoms which allow for individual effort and voluntary charity.

Other articles attempt to prove that government enterprise is always more inefficient and less rational than private enterprise. Comparing the workings and profits of American commercial airlines with nationalized European airlines, The Freeman cites results which are favorable toward the American system as proof that free enterprise gives rise to more efficiently and profitably run businesses. Other articles advance the view that the Social Security system "must fail."

The Freeman also contains philosophical discussions presenting the libertarian point of view. In "From Eden to Paradise, Choice vs. Compulsion" the author points out that a distinction must be made between "legal" and "moral." He develops this theory at length and applies it to the question of integration, claiming that discrimination based upon race may be morally wrong but it cannot be legally prevented without encroaching severely upon an individual's personal freedom. The author attacks the churches for attempting to "legislate morality." Another writer presents a series of articles about utopian visions and the relation of the "amelioristic reformers" of earlier centuries to the "hopeless" Marxists of a later era. The author attempts to illustrate the unreality inherent in all these schemes for reform.

Articles on foreign policy in The Freeman advocate isolationist policies and denounces foreign aid and involvement in the United Nations.

Editor's Response:
No approval or disapproval of the review was expressed in the reply from the editor.

The Gospel Truth

Address: P.O. Box 1144
          Oklahoma City, Oklahoma
Monthly; financial donations
Circulation: 6,000

Publication Started: 1938
Format: 6-page Newsletter
Issues Examined: November 1965, and January, February 1966

The Gospel Truth is a publication with religious orientation that deals in part with political issues from a moral or Bible prophetic standpoint." It is strongly anti-Communist, anti-U.N., and anti-National Council of Churches.

One of the articles by the editor, Rev. David F. Webber, quoted Korean exile Kilsoo Haan as stating that Russia and China "have cleverly thought out a phony rift to lure the West into a false sense of security," which may lead to a nuclear attack on the U. S.

The newsletter claims that the Supreme Court has made pro-Communist decisions. Cited are the overruling of the law prohibiting Communists from holding office in labor unions and free mail delivery of Communist propaganda from abroad. The editor states, in a letter, that "Our main objection to the National Council of Churches is its attempt to interpret the proper Christian attitude on social and political issues for its affiliate members." Among such issues are the admission of Red China to the U. N. and "obscene" literature.

The welfare programs of the Federal Government and the U. N. also come under attack. "It is immoral and unconstitutional for the government to gouge money from the rest of us to subsidize indolence, fornication, unwed motherhood, crime, agricultural overproduction, government 'art' rents ad stealum."

Each issue contains a sermon-like article by Dr. David Webber, a page entitled "My Patch of Blue" by Mrs. E. F. Webber, a column entitled "What Value Do We Place In a Child?", and "A Look At The Book" by Dr. Bob Jones Jr., in addition to the editorials previously mentioned.

Grass Roots

Address: Box 931
        San Angelo, Texas 76901
Monthly; $3.00 per year, 25¢ per copy.
Circulation:

Publication Started: 1953
Format: 10- to 16-page mimeographed Newsletter
Issues Examined: August, October, and November, 1965

Grass Roots calls itself "An independent monthly journal dedicated to a scientific study of the trends--'Digging down to the grassroots and coming up with paydirt'--Propagating the theology-philosophy of Kristology. Official organ of the Grassroots Movement."

One of the motivating concerns of Grass Roots is the editor's fear of Trotskyism. Rather than warning against communism in general, he usually speaks of the danger of Trotsky communism. "Trotsky Communism is a very live, dangerous thing today, both in Europe and in all the world--for they are everywhere. . . . I would really like to read just one thing that some senator, or Congressman, or governor, or newspaper columnist or news commentator or any other one of our many shining lights who promise so much for the show and present so little for the showdown--of what he or she has published, or written, or said against Trotsky Communism."

An anti-Jewish orientation is also very evident. "The Judaism of the Old Testament teaches lying, stealing, murdering, adultery, incest, and even selling rotten meat to 'thy neighbor' for food--teaches all these things as virtues--Jew virtues! I cannot go along with all that. So when I say I am anti-Jewish, I mean I am anti-Judaism, and this Judaism includes Zionism also."

This anti-Jewish feeling is linked with the editor's fear of Communism.

He says, "The Zionists hate the Russians and are seeking ways and means of overthrowing the Russian government and State, just as they hate the Americans and are seeking ways and means of destroying this country and taking it over. Hence it is the judaine (Judaism considered a poison) lurking in Russian Communism which marks it as the international treason, the enemy destroyer of all civilizations."

The editor seems to oppose the present Administration, calling the Great Society the "Gritty Society" and writing satirically about such programs as Medicare.

He also seems to oppose the militant civil rights movement, although he does not seem to be anti-Negro. Using parables, he speaks of "sit-ins, freedom-rioters and the Watts apes" as weeds and briars that need to be chopped down so that one can get at the edible vegetables among them.

Grass Roots treats a great variety of other subjects, e.g. dreams, censorship, Nietzsche, the origin of Christ, Voltaire, Jack Ruby, Lincoln's Gettysburg Address, and Queen Esther. The periodical consists of short, numbered paragraphs ("chapters") each dealing with a different subject. Sketches, poems, and excerpts from books are sometimes included.

Editor's Response:

"Generally speaking, a very good appraisal if you allow the corrections." (The corrections consisted of two suggested changes in verbatim quotations from Grass Roots, one of which was a change from the phrase "Watts apes" to "Watts Ghetto underbrush" in No. 161, Oct. 1965, page 2, line 12; the other one was the addition, to a quotation, of the words "Communism with you and me," which did not appear in the original text. The editor also added the designation "Trotsky" to the word "Communism" wherever it appeared, explaining that Lenin nicknamed Trotsky as "Judas Trotsky").

The Greater Nebraskan

Address: 1330 Turner Boulevard
         Omaha 5, Nebraska
Quarterly; $3.00 per year
Circulation: 1,000

Publication Started: 1923
Format: 20-page Magazine
Issues Examined: Spring, Summer, and Christmas 1965

The Greater Nebraskan takes a conservative stand in all the topics it deals with. An example is its opinion with regard to Federal Aid: "Governments have no money, states have no money, only people have money; therefore, Federal Aid is nothing but a myth." The magazine is a publication of The Congress of Freedom. At the 1965 meeting of the Congress, the following stands were "reaffirmed": that the U.S. withdraw from the U.N. and the U.N. headquarters be removed from the U.S.; that state legislatures endorse the Liberty Amendment (which greatly reduces the Federal government taxing power); that foreign aid is unconstitutional and "a cause of poverty"; that the U.S. rigidly adhere to the Monroe Doctrine as "sound foreign policy"; that the Civil Rights Bill is unconstitutional and should be repudiated; that the U.S. return to the Gold Standard; that states have the "constitutional right" to pass right-to-work laws; and that "we deplore all deviations from our charter of government, the Constitution of the U.S."

Articles appear on a number of current topics, many reprinted from other publications such as the Summit Sun of Mississippi and the Southwest Virginia Enterprise. One reprinted article, in the Spring issue, from Issues and Studies, a monthly publication from Taiwan, concerns Red China. It states that due to the agricultural and economic problems in the country, Red China still poses no great threat and that "any shift of our present policy toward Communist China in the form of appeasement will lead us not to settlement but to more confusion and chaos..."

The view with regard to race is summed up in the statement that "the Negro race cannot be taken as a group comprised of trustworthy people." The publication also recommends the impeachment of Earl Warren because "his unconstitutional usurpation of law-making power is a matter of record and cannot be considered 'good behavior.'" There is some Christian orientation to the magazine, but it appears mainly in the Christmas issue.

Heads Up

Address: P.O. Box 559
         Oroville, California 95965
Monthly; $3.00 per year
Circulation: Not ascertained

Publication Started: 1962 (?)
Format: 4-page Newsletter
Issues Examined: June, August
   (special edition), 1965

Heads Up describes itself as a "monthly anti-Communist newsletter" published by Karl Prussion, "a former Communist and FBI undercover operative." At present Prussion is a radio commentator. His daily news broadcast is also entitled "Heads Up."

Articles in Heads Up often urge readers to write their Congressmen and press for legislative investigation of Communists and Communist accommodators. The journal also encourages readers to engage in intensive political activity and help elect conservatives dedicated to fighting Communism.

The June 1965 newsletter contains articles entitled "Reuther Bids for Power," which maintains that "Martin 'Lucifer' King controls Reuther, who, in turn controls the White House"; "Supreme Court Opens Flood Gate to Red Propaganda"; "Prussion Challenges Martin Luther King"; and "Synanon Warning," which contends that the purpose behind Synanon Corporation's attempt to cure drug addiction is the control of society by an "elite class of Socialists." In August a special edition of Heads Up covers the story of the Los Angeles riots, under the heading, "Watts Insurrection-Result of Communist Civil Rights Movement."

The Herald of Freedom

Address: P.O. Box 3
         Zarepath, New Jersey
Biweekly: $10.00 per year
Circulation: Not ascertained

Publication Started: 1962
Format: 4-page Newsletter
Issues Examined: Several issues 1965

The Herald of Freedom is a four page newsletter representing the views and opinions of Frank A. Capell, editor and publisher. According to Mr. Capell, it is circulated in "50 states and 12 foreign countries, used by other publications and radio programs as News Feature Service." Each issue of the newsletter concentrates on a single topic. In one issue, Mr. Capell reviews the past history and qualifications of Abe Fortas, President Johnson's nominee for the Supreme Court seat vacated when Arthur Goldberg became the U.S. Ambassador to the United Nations. Capell attacks Fortas' record of cooperation with New Deal administrations, of his defense of, and association with, Communists, and his too close association with President Johnson. In another issue, "Part II" of "Christianity in Peril" is presented. It deals with anti-Catholicism, pointing out that the conservative Christians of all denominations must cooperate; first, because they are already outnumbered in the world and must not weaken their position further by internal division: "Christians who are willing to defend their religion are outnumbered 12 to 1," and secondly, because Christians must unite against their "mortal enemy," Communism.

Editor's Response:
    Editor expressed no disapproval.

Human Events

Address: 410 First Street, S.E.
         Washington, D.C. 20003
Weekly; $12.50 per year
Circulation: about 100,000

Publication Started: 1944
Format: 16-page tabloid Newspaper
Issues Examined: August 28, September 18, and 25, 1965

Human Events, a weekly newspaper, looks "at events through eyes that are biased in favor of limited constitutional government, local self-government, private enterprise and individual freedom." It contains three regular features: "This Week in Washington," "Capitol Camera," and "Spotlight on Congress." It also includes articles by a wide array of conservative syndicated columnists, as well as reprinted editorials from the nations' conservative newspapers.

"This Week in Washington" covers the major news events. Discussing the Watts riots, the column contends that they were caused by activities of civil rights groups, the Black Muslims, and organized street groups rather than by poverty and Negro ghetto conditions. The item "Abject Surrender to the U.N." discusses the Administration's ceasing to demand that the USSR and other delinquent nations pay their U.N. assessments.

"Capitol Camera" focuses mainly on Congress, particularly on statements made by legislators and on legislative action. Representative Roudebush (R - Ind.) scoffs at the Administration's spurious attempts at economical measures. The column also reports that General Curtis LeMay (Ret.) is "dismayed" at the new Air Force Secretary who, insiders remark, sides with McNamara's decision to scrap all manned bombers.

"Spotlight on Congress," a collection of items written by national legislators indicating their opinions on current issues, includes Sen. Harry Byrd's (D - Va.) claims that the repeal of the "right-to-work" provision of the Taft-Hartley Act would betray a fundamental liberty of the individual.

Columnists also criticize the policies of the present Administration. Morrie Ryskind writes that the President may achieve a "Great Society" but not a free society, and Barry Goldwater maintains that raising the minimum wage will hurt the poor by pricing marginal jobs out of existence.

Editor's Response:
Editor expressed no disapproval.

Imua Spotlight

Address: 568 Alexander Young Building
Honolulu, Hawaii 96813
Semimonthly (or monthly). Free to educational institutions
Circulation: 5,000

Publication Started: 1950
Format: Small size, 4- to 16-page Magazine
Issues Examined: Dec. 1965, Feb. 1966, Mid-Feb. 1966

Imua Spotlight is published by the Hawaii Foundation for American Freedoms, Inc. Its program is to "combat Communism and all subversive activities," to "live and work together in racial harmony," and to "demonstrate and maintain the American way of life." In the issues examined, the prevalent theme is that of anti-Communism. However, Imua aims not to "engage in blind, doctrinaire anti-Communism." Vice-President Jay Field states that "we have not fallen into the error of holding controversy automatically under suspicion. When we do use the label Communist against any group or individual, we guide ourselves by findings of courts and legislative, executive or judicial publications."

Not much editorial comment is given in Imua Spotlight. Articles and quotes from foreign news releases are concerned with Communist activities in both the U.S. and foreign countries. Examples are: "Anti-Communist revolts have spread through Tibet in 1965, much to the discomfort of the Peiping regime;" and "the merger of the Thai Independence Movement and the Thai Patriotic Front, masterminded by Peiping, marked a new insidious step by Chinese Communists in imitating and subverting Thailand..." Concerning Communist movements in the U.S., Imua printed an article about a summer camp set up by "American Communists" in Camp Midvale, New Jersey, which was a "Communist training school" for the "future leaders of the Communist Party, U.S.A."

In the mid-February 1966 issue, which is entirely devoted to an article entitled "The Soviet Role in Vietnam," Senator Thomas Dodd of Connecticut states that "so long as Hanoi refuses to call off its aggression, we should give the Saigon government the green light to organize hit-and-run raids and guerilla activities directed against the North... we should take the initiative in organizing a free world embargo on all shipments of grain to... Communist nations. Even if we ourselves had to buy the grain... I would be in favor of doing so... it would reduce the cost of war in terms of human life."

Editor's Response:
"Your evaluation of the Imua Spotlight as being substantially addressed to the issue of Communism is correct. I would like to add, however, that the two other points listed on the front of the Imua Spotlight are not neglected (See second sentence of first paragraph).

In A Nutshell

Address: 626 South Federal St.
(as of June 27, 1966)
Chicago, Ill. 60605
Monthly; Contributions only
Circulation: Cannot be divulged

Publication Started: 1947
Format: 16- to 20- 5 x 7 1/2" pages.
Also frequent 4- to 8- page supplement titled Facts for Freedom
Issues Examined: Vol. 18 No. 11, Vol. 18 No. 12, Vol. 19 No. 1 (no dates)

It is the belief of the editors of In A Nutshell that "this nation is being led down the road to a socialistic, controlled, bureaucratic, welfare state at an ever-increasing speed. If it continues, it must inevitably become totalitarian." Examples that it gives of the socialistic trend are that the judicial branch of the government has usurped legislative power, "state sovereignty has been practically erased," schools are coming under increasing Federal control, "banking has lost its independence," and "the state militia is almost a thing of the past."

The magazine is deeply concerned with the Communist infiltration of American life. One article states "many unions... are still under Communist influence," and cites the American Communication Association, The United Electrical Workers, and the West Coast Longshoremans' Union. The New York City Transit strike was termed a "Communist conspiracy," and an editorial spoke against the shipping of food and equipment to Communist countries quoting U.S. Rep. Lipscomb who said, "Apparently (some believe) we can feed and fight the Communists at the same time. I emphatically disagree."

Regarding the war in Vietnam, the publication wants Congress to take action. If Congress made a formal declaration of war, "the aid and trade we give the enemy" would be "treason," we could "blockade others aiding the enemy, and possibly the Republic of Free China would be allowed to enter the war."

In an article on Rhodesia, the editor asserts that there is still a high degree of illiteracy in the country and perhaps the country might not be ready for democracy yet; thus our insistence "on turning control of that country over to people not competent to govern" would be a "tragedy to whites and blacks alike."

The magazine consists mainly of editorials dealing with topics like those discussed above from a Conservative viewpoint. Also scattered throughout are humorous anecdotes on both political and non-political topics.

There is a small 4-8 page supplement to In A Nutshell called Facts for Freedom which has similar content to In A Nutshell. This appears at least six times a year.

Editor's Response:
Editor expressed no disapproval.

The Independent American

Address: P.O. Box 4223
New Orleans 18, Louisiana
"Published approximately every four to six weeks"; $3.00 per year
Circulation: 50,000

Publication Started: 1954
Format: 8-page Newsletter
Issues Examined: January-February; March-April; May-June 1965

The Independent American is a newspaper "dedicated to the defeat of Socialist and Communist influence that now pervade the thinking and the major policies of our Federal Government and the two major political parties." The journal emphatically states that there is a need for a new political party. William Loeb, in a reprint from the Manchester (N.H.) Union Leader, explains that the GOP is under liberal control, yet millions of people exist who think conservatively and basically disagree with the aims and philosophies of both major political parties. Joe Norman in "New Party Official Answers Critical Editorial" states that at present there is no party of opposition, since the Republican Party is in the hands of Scranton, Romney, and Company.

Publisher Kent Courtney in "Groundwork Laid for Anti-Communist Party" states that during the three-day meeting of the Congress of Conservatives in Chicago (chaired by Courtney), an Advance Committee was established to encourage the formation of new political parties at the state level.

The Independent American attacks foreign aid and loans, as well as trade with Communist countries. Congressman Glenard Lipscomb in "Trading with our Enemies" states that trade with Communist nations "will enable them to purchase selectively from the U.S. what they need and further their goal for world domination."

Negro demonstrations and Negro leaders are also criticized. Luke Greene's article, "Are Street Mobs Running the U.S.?", a reprint from the Atlanta Times; claims that "it wasn't the absence of legal means to secure the vote that led to the Alabama mobs, but a desire to punish a particular state and its public officials."

The Independent American attacks the present Congress and Administration on a variety of issues. A reprint, "Just Plain Dishonest," charges that the House of Representatives is dishonest in making cuts in the main budget and then passing supplementary appropriation bills. Edith Kermit Roosevelt's article, "What are they Trying to Hide?" contends that the U.S. security and intelligence services are infiltrated by Communists. Fulton Lewis, Jr. attacks Robert McNamara for "persistent disregard of the Joint Chiefs of Staff" and states that McNamara's refusal to proceed with the military space program threatens the nation's security and its very existence.

Editor's Response:
"I note that these comments cover three issues of our paper that were published in 1965. It is always interesting to me to review past issues of the paper because it points up so graphically how consistent is the editorial policy of The Independent American. Such consistency of course should not be surprising inasmuch as our paper is dedicated to a return to Constitutional principles - a constant if there ever was one!

"I have no opposition to your using the comments you submitted or any others which may be added inasmuch as we also are devout believers in freedom of the press and freedom to express one's opinion."

Inform - National Reports

Address: Inform
P. O. Box 489
Elizabeth, New Jersey
Monthly (variably dated)
Circulation: "We do not release these figures"

Publication Started: 1918 (as National Republic; became Inform-National Reports in 1960)
Format: 4-page Newsletter
Issues Examined: Nov. 11, Dec. 20, 1965, Jan. 19, 1966

The major aim behind the editorial staff of Inform is to uncover and combat subversive organizations in the U.S. In the issues examined all the articles are aimed toward anti-communism. As examples: In the November issues appears an article dealing with Castro's allowing dissatisfied Cubans to leave Cuba. Inform sees this as a "three cornered secret deal... worked out between the Department of State, Moscow and Castro." This will put Castro in as appearing more responsible, so that more friendly relations may be resumed with the U.S. In the December issue, the main article is entitled "Leprosy on Our Campuses"; it discusses the protest movements taking place among college students. Inform believes that these students "were subverted by some professor... working night and day... to pervert a whole generation to Socialism, Communism, Pacifism, and Defeatism."

The January issue contains an article concerning the Supreme Court, which Inform sees as aiding the Communists through its recent decisions. It describes the Supreme Court as Communism's "one sure haven of refuge."

Other stands taken by the newsletter include: seeing the new Panama

Canal agreement as "a monstrous sellout of United States security and interests"; advocating a definite position of policy to be taken in Vietnam, as the President has no right to send Americans "to battle for undefined and nebulous objectives"; and opposing trade with Communist nations. The issues of the newsletter that were examined contain articles mainly of an editorial nature.

Editor's Response:
"The summary was well written..."

The Kansas Free Lance

Address: P.O. Box 1777
Topeka, Kansas
Weekly; $8.00 yearly (20¢ per copy)
Circulation: 800

Publication Started:
Format: 4-page tabloid Newspaper
Issues Examined: Jan. 8, 15, and 22, 1965

The Kansas Free Lance is a conservative publication of "libertarian policy," emphasizing the importance of free enterprise, individual freedom, and states' rights... the Lance policy is a matter of championing the individual's right of choice in living his own life, and no exceptions granted." The editor states that "Intensity of desire is sufficient to win and establish a free society, but its endurance will depend on the depth of understanding of the nature of individual freedom."
The Kansas Free Lance opposes our present "welfare state" government, including our "socialistic" farm program, income tax, medicare, and labor unions. It opposes moderate Republican leaders of the "Lindsay-type... which identified with nothing, declares for nothing, and only appeals through television charm... a wishy-washy, warmed-over mess of spinach." It also opposes the moderate Republicans for "berating the John Birch Society and playing puppet for Liberal Establishment puppeteers." It opposes all forms of socialism and communism. The Kansas Free Lance sees former days as better than our own: "There was an intensely meaningful awareness of the value of individual freedom in yester-year's America." Generally, The Kansas Free Lance contains regular weekly features such as editorials, excerpts from periodicals, letters, and a column of miscellaneous comment. It deals largely with American domestic policy, not limiting itself to Kansas affairs.

Editor's Response:
"... your summation of our purpose and policy, while fairly and competently made, falls a little short of up-to-date accuracy. The fault is ours, not yours, for the most part." (Text updated as per suggestion.)

Keeping the Record Straight

Address: Edith Essig
    5938 W. Pasadena Avenue
    Glendale, Arizona 85301
Monthly; $2.50 per year
Circulation: 1,000

Publication Started: 1952
Format: 2- to 5-page Newsletter
Issues Examined: March 1, April 2, and May 1, 1966

In her newsletter, Edith Essig combines editorials written by herself with editorials from other publications such as The Arizona Republic and short news items from newspapers ranging from the London Daily Express to the Evening Dispatch of Columbus, Ohio to the B'nai B'rith Messenger, covering a wide range of current topics with editorial comments added occasionally. In turn, her editorials appear in other publications such as Candour: The B'rith Views Letter.

In each of the newsletters, Miss Essig subtly includes anti-Jewish remarks. For example, in her March editorial, she refers to "the trigger-happy Jewish manhunters;" in May, she states that "Zionist hopes of world control enter in Palestine where a time bomb has been ticking since a vast Arab population was robbed of its homeland to make way for the Jewish state..."

A Christian orientation is present in the writing witnessed by references to Bible passages. In her May editorial, she refers to the United States as a "Christian Republic" and mentions "our flag" and "the cross of Christ" as being "under heavy fire from a common enemy." She supports her statement that the U.S. is a "Christian Republic" with the facts that "The Founding Fathers of our Republic were all Christians" and "the U.S. Constitution declares its Christian Character." She also refers to the use of the Christian calendar and the fact that office holders such as Arthur Goldberg take "only half an oath, with hand on the Old Testament." She further states that "The First Article on the Bill of Rights prohibiting establishment of religion by Congress---that is, a state church as in England---quite evidently had reference to any one of various denominations of the Christian faith."

In the May issue, strong anti-internationalism was expressed: "... Patriots of the old breed have traced the intentions of those who hold the world's purse strings and have led us from one international crisis to another, in the stealthy lowering of the Stars and Stripes... and the endless schemes slanted toward world government along with this." Miss Essig expresses dislike of the U.N., remarking that the U.N. flag carries a "Design so similar to the great seal of the Soviet Union that it requires only the addition of the hammer and sickle to complete it."

Editor's Response:
    Editor expressed no disapproval.

Liberty Letter

Address: 300 Independence Avenue,
         S. E.
         Washington, D. C. 20003
Monthly during Congressional sessions:
$1.00 per year
Circulation: 175,000

Publication Started: 1960
Format: 4-page Newsletter
Issues Examined: May, June, Sept. 1965

Liberty Letter is a publication of the Liberty Lobby and its purpose is to inform its readers concerning legislation under consideration in Congress and to urge them to write letters supporting or opposing certain measures. The stands taken by the publication include: opposition to medicare, reduction of foreign aid, opposition to Communist trade expansion and the consular treaty allowing Soviet consulates to open up in major American cities, and opposition to the proposed repeal of the right-to-work law under the Taft-Hartley Act.

Liberty Letter opposes any increase in immigration quotas and proposes that immigration be suspended "during periods of 3.5% unemployment except to reunify families to a first degree blood relationship."

In the May issue is an article entitled "Black Revolution is Red Revolution" in which it expresses the belief that the Negro movement is manipulated by the Communist infiltration tactics. Liberty Letter states: "History shows that in every country marked for Communist conquest the tactics are the same ---- use cannon fodder from groups which feel exploited. Supply slogans and leadership... get the support of liberals... and the result is predictable." Martin Luther King is described as having "been a member of, or unwittingly accepted support from over 60 Communist fronts..."

The same issue also has an article entitled "The Trial of Everett M. Dirksen" in which the senator is described as having "betrayed the confidence of the 27 million Americans who voted for the conservative candidate that he himself placed in nomination in 1964." The basis of this betrayal is his support of the sale of wheat to Cuba, the Test-Ban Treaty, the Civil Rights Act of 1964, and the Voting Rights Act of 1965.

Each issue examined contains a column entitled "Legislative Outlook" giving the Liberty Lobby's opinions on the bills in Congress. Also included besides the editorial articles are news items concerning Conservative activities, and suggestions concerning books the readers might be interested in.

Editor's Response:
"O. K."

Life Lines (now <u>Freedom Talks</u>)

Address: 4330 N. Central Exprwy.
         Dallas, Texas 75206
Daily: 32 wks; $4.00. 52 wks; $5.00
Circulation: 18,000

Publication Started: 1959
Format: 4-page Newsletter
Issues Examined: Feb. 8, May 17, 22, and June 3, 10 1966

<u>Life Lines</u> is the transcript of a daily radio broadcast made by Melvin Munn in Washington, D.C. Each one deals with a topic of current interest covering subjects ranging from foreign policy to problems of federal-domestic policy and private life. There is a strong orientation toward religious belief and anti-communism.

The February 9 broadcast deals with the discussion of two policies---the idea of privileged sanctuary and non-intervention. Privileged sanctuary concerns the regarding of "organized territory of Communist enemies as inviolate from any form of military attack." It is stated that President Johnson's "air attacks in North Vietnam in 1965 signaled a decisive break" with the doctrine, but that now a new sanctuary termed "the red envelope" has developed. <u>Life Lines</u> states: "official reasons given for not attacking this area suggest... the thinking of the kind of mind which cringes at the slightest hint of 'adverse world opinion' and regards American lives as more expendable than the good will of foreign nations." Concerning non-intervention, it says "The very thought of American intervention brings howls of outrage. But Communist intervention... is dismissed with a shrug."

In a discussion of the poverty programs of the government May 17, 1966, <u>Life Lines</u> states: "By the standards of most of the world, even our poverty is undreamed of wealth." And it sees "socialism and communism all over the world" as "gravely (threatening) our American liberties." In the June 3 broadcast in reference to withdrawal from Vietnam, Mr. Munn states: "...if we were to withdraw, at this time, we would be portrayed in the eye of the world as a paper tiger... we would demonstrate to the world that the American commitment is meaningless..." The June 10 broadcast is concerned with college demonstrations for "free speech." Mr. Munn gives, in this article, a digest of a speech by Dr. W. P. Shofstall, Dean of Students at Arizona State University. Dr. Shofstall states that many people, "especially pseudo intellectuals, minority groups and new nations--are demanding the freedom to do as they please" rather than to do as they should. So, the slogans 'academic freedom and free speech' are used as an excuse by the students to engage in 'temper tantrums' called 'demonstrations' or 'protests'."

Manion Forum

Address: St. Joseph Bank Building
        South Bend, Indiana
Weekly; $5.00 per year
Circulation: Not ascertained

Publication Started: 1955
Format: 4-page Newsletter
Issues Examined: May 16, 1965; January 2, 9, and 16, 1966

The Manion Forum, a weekly radio broadcast in which Clarence Manion, former Dean of the Notre Dame University Law School, interviews noted conservative figures, is reprinted as a newsletter also entitled Manion Forum. Each issue is devoted to an interview with one person on a single topic.

In the January 2, 1966 issue, Fred Schlafly an Illinois lawyer and member of the American Association's Special Committee on Communist Tactics, Strategy, and Objectives, is interviewed concerning Communism and the Supreme Court. Mr. Schlafly reviews a report of this committee which dealt with "Recent decisions of the U.S. Supreme Court in cases involving national and state security and with particular reference to Communist activities . . . ," showing how these decisions have weakened U.S. security and aided the Communist cause. Mr. Schlafly also discusses similar Supreme Court decisions made since the appearance of the Special Committee Report. An example of the sort of case he discusses is U.S. vs. Seager, in which the Supreme Court allowed a young man to be considered a conscientious objector in spite of the fact that he belonged to no religious group. Mr. Schlafly comments that "Pacifist and pro-Communist organizations were quick to exploit the hole driven by the Supreme Court in the Selective Service Act."

In the January issue, Jules Dubois, Latin American Correspondent for the Chicago Tribune, is interviewed concerning the relationship between communism and U.S. intervention in the Dominican Republic. Mr. Dubois deplores the deportation from the Dominican Republic of General Wessin y Wessin, "the foremost anti-Communist in the country," and predicts the election of Juan Bosch and the eventual delivering of the Dominican Republic to the Communists. Mr. Manion and Mr. Dubois see this trend as part of a pattern of "Communist-directed activities all over Latin America."

Editor's Response:
    Editor expressed no disapproval.

The Mindszenty Report

Address: P.O. Box 321, Clayton
　　　　 Branch
　　　　 St. Louis, Missouri 63105
Monthly; $2.00 per year
Circulation: Not ascertained

Publication Started: 1958 (entitled
　Release until 1962)
Format: 4-page Newsletter
Issues Examined: July and August,
　1965

　　The Mindszenty Report, a monthly newsletter published by the Cardinal Mindszenty Foundation which describes itself as "a non-profit, educational organization whose purpose is to combat Communism with knowledge and facts," strives to dispel apathy and to alert Catholics to the danger of Communism. Issues reviewed contain reports on activities, news and feature articles, and book reviews. The July 1965 issue contains an article entitled "Communists on College Campuses," a review of Kenneth Colegrave's Democracy versus Communism and a report on a new organization--the Veritas Committee on Pacem in Terris--whose purpose is to counteract the misuse of Pope John's Encyclical on the subject. The August 1965 report contains excerpts from Rev. Anthony Gliozzo's "long and scholarly treatise" on "Pope Paul's Mandate to the Jesuits," which was to "combat atheism." Charles Cardinal Journet of Switzerland defends the "moral position of peace through strength" in "The Christian Conscience Faced with the Nuclear Weapon," an article in the same issue.

Minute Women

Address: 25 Forest Road
　　　　 Wheeling, West Virginia
　　　　 26003
Monthly first four months of the year;
　bimonthly thereafter; $3.00 per
　year
Circulation: Not ascertained

Publication Started: 1953
Format: 4-page Newsletter
Issues Examined: April, May/June,
　1965

　　The Minute Women of the U.S.A. publish a monthly newsletter for the purpose of keeping their membership informed about "the frightening advance of socialism and bureaucracy which threatens the future of this nation as a constitutional Republic." The Minute Women describe their organization as non-partisan, non-sectarian and educational. They stand for ten basic principles: belief in God, belief in the Christian principles embodied in the Constitution of the United States, states rights, economy and efficiency in government, clean politics, a sound dollar, fairer taxes, free enterprise, a courageous and enlightened foreign policy, and patriotic teaching in our schools and colleges. Concern for these principles is reflected in their newsletter.

The newsletter begins with an open letter to the members of the Minute Women organization from their national chairman at present, Dorothy B. Frankston. She fashions her comments around a series of quotations. In the April 1965 issue, she attempts to focus the attention of all Minute Women on alleged violations of the Constitution through the improper use of authority by the Executive and Legislative branches of the Government. "The paramount task of this 89th Congress is simply the defense of its dwindling powers and declining prerogatives, and the recapture of those already fallen into the hands of the White House and Supreme Court."

In addition to the letter from the national chairman, the newsletter contains discussions of numerous books, pamphlets, Congressional reports, and magazine and newspaper articles. A wide range of subjects is covered in the issues examined. <u>Treason is the Reason</u>, by Frank A. Capell; <u>Where's the Rest of Me?</u>, by Ronald Reagan; <u>Negroes with Guns</u>, by Robert F. Williams; and a pamphlet entitled "Communism, Hypotism and the Beatles," by David A. Noebel, are among titles reviewed.

The newsletter urges Minute Women to take action--to write their Congressmen, to vote, and to inform others. They are also reminded always to speak as individuals and never as "Minute Women." Further, each Minute Woman is asked to take only that action which her conscience dictates.

Editor's Response:

"I find the summary . . . quite well done. There are many additions I could make but since I know it must be concise and cover the territory as briefly as possible I feel it does that job pretty well as it is."

Modern Age

Address: 154 East Superior Street
        Chicago, Illinois 60611
Quarterly; $4.00 per year
Circulation: 6,000

Publication Started: 1957
Format: 100-page Magazine
Issues Examined: Fall, 1964; Spring and Summer, 1965

<u>Modern Age</u>, an erudite journal favoring an intellectual, conservative viewpoint, focuses upon the evils of depersonalization in a "welfare-oriented" society. Charles Wilson's study of "The New Generation of Private Colleges" emphasizes the freedom of the independent college from "politicians' chicanery" as well as its role in saving the tax payer money by drawing on private resources and by avoiding the "froths and fizzes of the old rah-rah-varsity spirit." Moreover, Wilson points out that the

private colleges are streaking ahead of the huge state-supported institutions in terms of scholarship. Robert L. Cunningham's "The Redefinition of Work: A look at automation and utopia" centers on the thesis of The Triple Revolution, a document signed by thirty-four American intellectual leaders, which discusses the relation between automation and resulting unemployment and advocates a guaranteed annual income for all. Cunningham attempts to "point to and underline certain verbal confusions and errors of analysis which make it difficult to accept as well founded much of what is said in the document."

Articles show intense criticism of both communist and fascist movements, often presenting historical studies of totalitarian movements in the twentieth century.

Modern Age also features discussions of literature, presenting book reviews as well as critical studies of literary works and figures. Titles range from Cleanth Brooks' William Faulkner: The Yoknapatawpha Country, reviewed by Louis Bredvold, to John Dos Passos' Occasions and Protests, studies by J. M. Lalley. Modern Age also includes poetry in many issues.

Other book reviews focus on political and historical subjects, including Peter J. Stanlis' discussion of Carl B. Cone's Burke and the Nature of Politics: The Age of French Revolution and Felix Morley's review of James J. Martin's American Liberalism and World Politics, 1931-1941, entitled "Apostasy of Liberalism."

Editor's Response:
"The statement you have prepared on Modern Age seems OK to us."

National Forecast

Address: National Forecast Ministry, Inc.
Topton, North Carolina
28781
Monthly (September through June);
$2.00 per year
Circulation: Not ascertained

Publication Started: 1941
Format: 20-page Magazine
Issues Examined: March, 1963; February, 1966

National Forecast is "dedicated to the interpretation of today's turmoil in the light of Divine Prophecy." The editor "has proclaimed that all heathen races of the earth (excluding Christian) will eventually embrace Communism and set themselves against Western Civilization." The publication stands against internationalism and one-world government" as being "an anti-God setup which would lead us all into ultimate slavery." It states that American salvation will come only through an "outside

Savior, and God's Christ is that Savior." The war in Vietnam is seen as a "philanthropic mission our people have undertaken."

The National Program Letter

Address: 900 East Center
    Searcy, Arkansas
Monthly; $1.00 per year
Circulation: 50,000

Publication Started: 1942 (as Harding College Letter)
Format: 4-page Newsletter
Issues Examined: March, 1965

The National Program Letter is published by the National Education Program, founded by Dr. George Benson of Harding College. The organization also sponsors forums, TV programs, radio broadcasts, films and tapes. Dr. Benson states that the Letter is devoted to "emphasizing to the American people the importance of our faith in God, the value of constitutional government and freedom of opportunity under a private enterprise economy." An article on "A Greater Society's Frontiers" discusses the national crime rate and moral erosion, appealing for a return to individual responsibility. "Cool Words and Hot Bullets" supports U.S. policy in Vietnam while "Why Not Speak Up?" encourages conservative Americans to speak out for what they believe in, especially in regard to the nation's economy. The journal also calls for stronger controls over Communist Party members in America and contains excerpts from a speech which Dr. Benson delivered to the 73rd Continental Congress of the Daughters of the American Revolution.

Editor's Response:
    "I am returning it [the summary] with no changes."

The New Guard

Address: 1221 Massachusetts Avenue,
    N.W. Suite A
    Washington, D.C. 20005
Monthly; $4.00 per year
Circulation: 25,000

Publication Started: 1961
Format: 24- to 30-page Magazine
Issues Examined: March through June, 1965; April and May, 1966

The New Guard is the news organ of the Young Americans for Freedom, which describes itself as America's "largest conservative organization for youth." The magazine gives considerable coverage of YAF activities. For example, it reports that YAF campaigning helped elect a conservative, anti-medicare Congressman in a district in Florida in which many retired people live; the journal views this election as evidence that the medicare program does not enjoy grassroots support. The editor states that "YAF is a political-activist and issues oriented group . . . while YAF is independent of the Republican Party or any other group, most of its members (and the magazine's readers) were enthusiastic supporters of Barry Goldwater . . . The New Guard, however, does not hesitate to support President Johnson or other Democrats on occasion where their views coincide."

The magazine features write-ups on young conservative leaders and politicians in America. Articles about domestic and foreign affairs also appear regularly. For example, in the April 1966 issue an article by Dr. William Jay Jacobs entitled "What's Happened to Patriotism?" criticized progressive educational techniques, blaming the new types of textbooks for the decline of patriotic spirit. Another article "Conservative Hari-Kari" by Donald J. Devine, criticised the Conservative Party of New York for being more concerned with being a party than with endorsing conservative candidates. In the May 1966 issue, an editorial opposes the U.N. Security Council's resolution on Rhodesia "authorizing Britain to use force to prevent oil-bearing ships from reaching the Mozambique port of Beira" as "illegal." Another article "The Fascist Threat to America" by Richard S. Wheeler states that "The thrust of modern liberalism's economic and political programs is toward an indigenous fascism . . . Fear not the black-shirts, but rather that mild-mannered Government man in the brown tweed suit."

The editor states that "usually there are a number of editorial paragraphs (short subjects), followed by two or three pages of full-length editorials. The emphasis is on foreign policy developments, domestic issues before Congress, and political development." Also included are one or two page articles, with emphasis "on political developments and issues. These are humor and how-to-do-it articles"; "YAF Washington Report" which is a "series of reports on developments within the Republican Party and studies of legislation before Congress"; book reviews; and "YAF Roundup," three to five pages of articles and pictures covering the activities of the YAF.

New Individualist Review

Address: Ida Noyes Hall
    University of Chicago
    Chicago, Illinois
Quarterly (irregular); $3.00 per year (students $1.50)
Circulation: 4,000

Publication Started: 1961
Format: 64-page Magazine
Issues Examined: Vols. I and II (1961-63); Vol. IV, No. 2 Winter 1966

The New Individualist Review, "a journal of classical liberal thought," espouses the principles of classical liberal thought and individualism (libertarianism). The editors "believe in free, private enterprise, and in the imposition of the strictest limits to the power of government." Articles express their viewpoints on contemporary issues, contrasting the libertarian with representatives of the New Left and New Right. The editor states that the publication makes "a determined effort to publish scholarly articles, i.e. by authors who have some presumed competence in their fields."

In the November 1961 issue, editor Ronald Hamowy presents a critique of the National Review, to which William F. Buckley, Jr. replies. Hamowy charges that the Right has abandoned its libertarian principles--"The great moral principle of individual liberty has been superseded by the arrogance of the pseudo-aristocrat who preserves his civilized airs by exploiting the serf labor of 'inferior' people; the libertarian principle of peace and nonintervention has been replaced by the heroics of a barroom drunk who proudly boasts that 'he can lick anybody in the room.'"

Buckley's three-part answer attempts to refute Hamowy's statement that the Right has become authoritarian; Buckley replies: "A conservative will argue for that system in a given country which will maximize freedom. But that system is not necessarily one that is based on one man, one vote; or even, necessarily, on the right of self-rule."

In the Winter 1966 issue, Murray N. Rothbard discusses the "Hoover Myth"--that Hoover was not a "politician," and was a great isolationist and individualist. He regards the myth as a "total misinterpretation, on all sides, of the Hoover record." Challenging this myth, he points out that Hoover "was a politician and cannot be allowed to escape the responsibility for his chosen profession." He was supported for the Democratic nomination for the Presidency in 1919 by left-wing Democrats, including Louis Brandeis, Herbert Croly, and Franklin D. Roosevelt. To disprove Hoover's individualism, Rothbard says that in 1912 Hoover supported Roosevelt's Progressive Party, "for Hoover had become the very model of an 'enlightened' left-wing Republican: and superficially his views might be called 'socialistic'; but it would be more precise to term them 'mercantilist' or 'state capitalist' . . . " As for Hoover's isolationism, Rothbard says, "by the spring of 1917, Hoover had gone over to the pro-war camp, and sent Wilson a warm telegram of congratulations for his war message."

The New Individualist Review discusses economics, concepts of freedom, and theories of educational institutions (in this latter, it recommends private schooling). It also includes book reviews and discussions of articles in other journals.

Editor's Response:
"The summary seems fair . . . ."

News and Views

Address: National Layman's Council
of the Church League of
America
422 North Prospect Street
Wheaton, Illinois
Monthly; price varies with issue
size
Circulation: Not ascertained

Publication Started: 1937
Format: 12- to 16-page Newsletter
Issues Examined: April and May,
1966

Each edition of News and Views is dedicated to one topic. The April issue is the third of a three-part article on the Soviet infiltration of the American culture. It is concerned with the educational system and how subversion is taking place in this area. "America's assorted radicals and rebels . . . began a massive assault on traditional values in religion, patriotism, art, entertainment, and morality," claims the publication. It cites "the pinko college professors" as being responsible for this. It calls the free universities "little more than Marxist discussion groups." The same article describes the Berkeley riots as "a national disgrace."

The May issue is a reprint (without editorial comment) of the 1920 report of the New York State Joint Committee on "Socialism and the Churches. In it is stated "unless this movement (Socialism) is killed and unless the Constructive movement of Church leaders leads to a revival of religious belief, the necessary foundations for permanent social reconstruction will be wanting." Also in the New York government report is the belief that the "denominational walls of separation" are important in spreading Christian beliefs.

Editor's Response:
Editor expressed no disapproval.

The Objectivist

Address: 120 East 34th Street
New York, New York 10016
Monthly; $5.00 per year (50¢ per
single copy)
Circulation: 21,056

Publication Started: 1962 (as The
Objectivist Newsletter); title
changed in 1966
Format: Small size, 20-page Magazine
Issues Examined: October, November and December, 1965

The Objectivist Newsletter is written in defense of capitalism. In the October issue, Ayn Rand, one of the editors, states in an article entitled "The Obliteration of Capitalism," "The liberals are coining and spreading 'anti-concepts' in order to smuggle this country into statism . . . and the primary target marked for obliteration is the concept of 'capitalism' which, if lost, would carry away with it the knowledge that a free society can and did exist." She defines capitalism as "the only system in history where wealth was not acquired by looting, but by production, not by force, but by trade, the only system that stood for man's rights to his own mind, to his work, to his life, to his happiness, to himself."

The November and December issues contain a two-part article, by Miss Rand, defining capitalism. She also explains objectivism, the ideology behind the publication. "The objective theory holds that the good is neither an attitude of 'things in themselves' nor of man's emotional states, but an evaluation of the facts of reality by man's consciousness according to a rational standard of value."

Also included in the issues examined are: a review of the book The Democrat's Dilemma by P. M. Crane in which the reviewer states: "It is particularly recommended to so-called 'political activists' who are eager to fight for capitalism . . . without any knowledge of what caused the collectivist trend . . ."; an article written by Nathaniel Brandon, co-editor of the newsletter, describing psychological maturity as meaning that "within the sphere of his first-hand concerns, of his own actions and zeals, (a genuinely mature adult) regards himself as competent to know that which he needs to know and he acquires whatever knowledge his interests and purposes demand."

Editor's Response:
"The article grossly misrepresents the purpose and general content of our publication in its stress on politics . . . I am, therefore, submitting entirely new copy, which will more accurately reflect the nature of our journal." See the following summary, covering the issues of January, March, April, and June of 1966:

The Objectivist is a monthly journal that deals with the theoretical aspects of Objectivism, with its application to modern problems, and with the evaluation of today's cultural trends. It is edited and published by the founder of Objectivism, novelist-philosopher Ayn Rand, and by Nathaniel Branden, a psychological theorist.

In the January 1966 issue, Ayn Rand states, in an article entitled "Altruism as Appeasement" that, in the field of politics, the more aggressive type of altruist-appeasers, the "liberals," believe in "rule by physical force . . . " and in the doctrine "people are unfit for freedom and should be ruled--'for their own good'--by a dictatorship of the 'elite.'" Miss Rand continues: "Hence such 'liberals'' tolerant sympathy for the regimes of Soviet Russia or Red China, and their appalling indifference to the wholesale atrocities of those countries."

In the March 1966 issue, Nathaniel Branden writes, in an article entitled "Volition and the Law of Causality": "Objectivism locates man's free will in a single action, in a single basic choice: to think or not to think. This choice--given the context of his knowledge and of the existential possibilities confronting him--controls all of man's other choices, and directs the course of his actions. The [Objectivist] concept of man as a being of violitional consciousness stands in sharp opposition to the view that dominates our culture in general and the 'social sciences' in particular: the doctrine of psychological determinism."

In the April 1966 issue, is a review of the book The Federal Bulldozer by Martin Anderson, in which the reviewer states that the book "offers a clearly reasoned and compelling case for the repeal of the urban renewal program," and recommends the book to "Those who seek an intelligible account of this federal program, or who are interested in studies dealing with the inefficiency of government intervention in the economy . . . ."

In the June 1966 issue, in an article entitled "The Roots of War," Ayn Rand writes: "Men are afraid that war might come because they know . . . they have never rejected the doctrine which causes wars . . . the doctrine that it is right or practical or necessary for men to achieve their goals by means of physical force (by initiating the use of force against other men) and that some sort of 'good can justify it." Miss Rand concludes the article with the statement: "Let all those who are actually concerned with peace . . . realize that if war is ever to be outlawed, it is the use of force that has to be outlawed."

Also in the June 1966 issue, in an article entitled "Emotions and Actions," Nathaniel Branden writes: "Contradictions cannot exist in reality. But a man can hold ideas, beliefs, values which . . . are contradictory . . . . The disastrous consequences of [man's] holding contradictory values--which is at the heart of neurotic anxiety--is the short-circuiting of [his] value-emotion-action mechanism . . . . Whether a man's emotional mechanism brings him happiness or suffering depends on its programming. It depends on the validity and consistency of his values . . . . According to the values [a man] selects, he makes the motivational power of his emotions work in the service of his life--or against it."

On Target

Address: P.O. Box 172
        Independence, Missouri
Monthly; $5.00 per year
Circulation: Not ascertained

Publication Started: 1963
Format: 8-page Newsletter
Issues Examined: May, 1965

On Target is the official publication of the Minutemen, an armed secret organization that seeks to combat Communism. Its motto is "Words Won't

Win--Action Will."

The May 1965 issue of On Target stresses the vastness of the problem facing patriots. In "The Madmen," David Woodbury discusses our nation's leaders: "This time we are faced, not by a simple maniac but by a new elite of mattoids--unbalanced but dangerously brilliant people--who are capable of using the totality of science and political knowledge against us and the world."

Using photographs extensively, On Target wishes to keep Minutemen informed about "subversive" individuals, movements, and organizations. The May 1965 issue contains the names and addresses of state officials of the United Nations Association, which On Target views as "nearly saturated with Communists and Fabian Socialists."

Our American Heritage Committee News Bulletin

Address: Our American Heritage
Committee
P.O. Box 60084
Oklahoma City, Oklahoma
73106
Monthly; $2.00 per year
Circulation: 773

Publication Started: 1963
Format: 12- to 16-page Newsletter
Issues Examined: December, 1965; January, 1966

Included in the OAHC (Our American Heritage Committee) News Bulletin are articles from other organizations, such as The Liberty Amendment Committee and Constitutional Alliance Inc. ("non-partisan . . . and dedicated to the nomination and election of Constitutionalists to public office"). These organizations have similar aims as those of OAHC--"to provide an organization for people of all ages and occupations to join together for the study and practice of traditional American Citizenship." OAHC sees our American heritage as consisting of "belief in God and the responsibility of each individual to God for his own welfare and self discipline," "individual ownership of property exchanged in a free market . . . . " and "a Constitutional Government limited to the mutual protection of citizens."

Anti-Communism is one of the major goals of OAHC and many articles deal with this theme. For example in December in "Is Modern Miracle-American Traditionalism Lost?" Leonard Reed, President of the Foundation of Economic Education, states that "a vast percentage of Americans today subscribe to and support the tenets of Communist philosophy." Some examples given by the author are "heavy progressive or graduated income tax; centralization of the means of Communication and transport in the hands of the state; and free education for all children in public schools." Also in this issue is "A Key to Communist Semantics" from the Canadian

-139-

Intelligence Service.

Each copy of the News Bulletin contains an article by a minister on the first page. In the January 1966 issue Anson Justice, a Baptist, advocated that regular church attendance was the way to show God appreciation for the American heritage. Each copy urges readers to write their Congressmen concerning certain bills under consideration. OAHC favors the bill to revoke U.S. membership in the U.N. and retention of 14-b of the Taft-Hartley law concerning the right-to-work. The organization opposes the bill to set up Soviet consulates in major American cities, on the basis that it would "allow the Kremlin to spread espionage centers across America under the thin guise of calling them 'consulates.'"

Editor's Response:
Editor expressed no disapproval.

The Plain Truth

Address: Box 111
        Pasadena, California 91109
Monthly; Free distribution
Circulation: 800,000

Publication Started: 1934
Format: 52-page Magazine
Issues Examined: November, December, 1965; January, 1966

The Plain Truth is a magazine published by Ambassador College, with emphasis on world events and scientific and religious problems. It represents a conservative position on world affairs, but its ideas do not always fit the typical right-wing pattern. Religious matters are of prime importance, and they determine this publication's position with respect to political issues. The uniqueness of its views is partly the result of the great emphasis placed on Biblical prophecies.

Many articles in this magazine indicate that its writers are as concerned about Germany as they are about Communism. They predict that Germany will regain power, eventually dominating a "United States of Europe" and causing World War III.

Another idea prevalent in The Plain Truth is that America and Britain are "the descendents of the ancient House of Israel," the modern "chosen people of God," recipients of both responsibilities and great material blessing. These chosen Anglo-Saxons, however, are guilty of increasing "crime, immorality, illicit sex, filth, perversion, race hatred, and violence." Because they are neglecting their God-given responsibilities, they are losing their power (e.g. Britain has lost the Suez; America is losing the Panama Canal) and are in danger of punishment by God in the form of World War III. The writers of The Plain Truth believe that "something is drastically wrong with civilization as we know it today--whether it be diabolical Communism or Fascism or the Western brand of civilization which we call democracy."

The typical pattern in this magazine is to report objectively on a world event, such as Pope Paul's U.N. visit, and then to comment on its significance in terms of religion and prophecy. Since this magazine is circulated all over the world, the events considered are usually world events rather than specifically American. Other articles comment on educational and social problems such as modern music or modern marriage. Each issue also contains a Bible story for children and adults.

Editor's Response:
"Grasp of content is fundamentally sound in student's mind."

Rampart Journal of Individual Thought

Address: Box 158
        Larkspur, Colorado 80118
Quarterly; $7.50 per year ($5.00 for students)
Circulation: 841 total, 787 paid

Publication Started: 1965
Format: Small size, 75- to 144-page Magazine
Issues Examined: Spring, Summer, Fall, Winter, 1965

Upholding a firm respect for private property and a distrust of strong, central government, Rampart Journal presents essays challenging high taxation and anti-poverty legislation and supporting a laissez-faire economy.

Robert LeFevre, who contributes to each issue in the column, "On the Other Hand," perhaps best voices the magazine's individualist philosophy in his article, "Autarchy Versus Anarchy." LeFevre defines freedom as "autarchy-self-rule" and maintains that "the autarchist is content to permit the market place to make its own adjustments or revisions, if and when they are needed." He favors "human liberty"; he believes in "property as a total concept," favors "moral fulfillment of contracts," and supports "profits, rents, and interest without equivocation." In another article, "The Stoic Virtues," LeFevre praises the fortitude of the stoic temper, asserting that "without a compelling urgency toward frugality, thrift and endurance, modern capitalism could never have been born."

Oscar W. Cooley's "What is Property?" presents several concepts of property and concludes in support of the view that property is control of things and "in order to live man must control himself and things about him," viewing life as "contingent upon property."

In one issue, Rampart Journal includes an article opposing the magazine's own editorial philosophy: Robert Clancy, director of the Henry George School of Social Science, presents "A Challenge to Libertarians" in response to LeFevre's "A Challenge to the Georgists."

The magazine also publishes book reviews on books supporting a conservative or libertarian stance.

Editor's Response:
"Your assistant has done a find job, in our opinion . . . . We are content with the copy as it stands."

Rank and File

Address: 210 Mohawk Building
        Portland, Oregon 97204
Occasionally; $3.00 per year
Circulation: Not ascertained

Publication Started: 1960
Format: Small size, 16-page Magazine
Issues Examined: October, November, 1965; January, 1966

Rank and File describes itself as "a conservative employee magazine, and welcomes . . . items of interest to patriotic workers who are concerned with furthering rank and file representation within their own unions. It also states that "an increasing number of employers . . . have taken it upon themselves to provide their people with Rank and File."

The publication takes a conservative stand on such problems as the war in Vietnam, which (it believes) should be more aggressive; the U.N., which it describes as "atheistic and amoral"; organized labor, which it terms a "political octopus"; and the AFL-CIO, which it describes as "the most powerful--and ruthless--political mafia this nation has known."

There is a strong prevailing theme of anti-Communism. Rank and File believes that "our Judaeo-Christian Civilization is engaged in a fight to the death with an atheistic, materialistic empire which in less than fifty years has gained control of forty percent of the world's population and twenty-five percent of its land mass." This statement comes from Lee J. Adamson in an article describing the name-calling that is going back and forth between certain rightist publications and groups. He goes on to say, "Nothing could better please the leaders of the global conspiracy that is international communism than these exhibitions of internecine warfare among its opponents."

Each of the issues examined contains editorials concerned with labor, Vietnam, and other current political and economic considerations. Cartoons are supplied throughout, satirizing the campus protester, the Johnson Administration, and Vietnam.

Editor's Response:
"We would like, in some respects, to think our effort is a counterpart of the labor press, and our fondest hope would be that the rank and file union members would be persuaded to extend themselves to attend their union meetings . . . and exercise their voting prerogatives to correct the

very abuses they so loudly condemn in their labor organizations.

"Approximately 23% of our subscriptions are provided by employers for their people; the balance are individuals for their friends or acquaintances. Each state is represented to some degree now, and 14 subscriptions in foreign countries."

The Review of the News

Address: 395 Concord Avenue
        Belmont, Massachusetts
        02178
Weekly; $10.00 per year ($20.00 via air mail)
Circulation: Not ascertained

Publication Started: 1965
Format: Small size, 32-page Magazine
Issues Examined: November 26, December 1, 1965; January 6-16, January 13-19, 1966

The Review of the News is a magazine which summarizes in capsule the daily news, analyzes important issues, and makes revisions according to its own viewpoint of news excerpts from other publications.

The Review of the News states its own policy thus: "This magazine will have but one axe to grind . . . truth. We will not slant, shade or hedge. We intend to offer hard news in concise, capsulated form . . . . We will avoid propaganda, and we will leave smart language to essayists in 'little magazines.' And we leave dishonesty for those who deem it valuable. We will not . . . manufacture support or 'news' for any of the myriad of ideological causes."

The news-reporting section of The Review of the News consists of very brief, one paragraph summaries without editorial comment. The orientation of Review of the News is seen in its choice of topics, such as, repeated reference to Negroes in civil rights agitation as "hundreds of rock-throwing Negro students," or "screaming Negroes" who "snarl traffic"; and repeated reference to various organizations, such as the Southern Conference Educational Fund, as "Communist Front."

And in the "Analysis and "Correction, Please!" sections of the magazine, it becomes apparent that this publication is right wing, anti-Communist, pro-McCarthy, and anti-U.N. For example, it analyzes the Dominican situation thus: "The most blatant pro-Communist move our government has so far performed in that Caribbean country was to expel Brigadier General Elias Wessin y Wessin." Concerning the Vietnam policy of the U.S., The Review of the News is in favor of intensifying the war in order to gain quick victory. It accuses President Johnson of encouraging opposition to "The John Birch Society, Ronald Reagan, and the Dan Smoot Report." It upholds the value of "capitalism, free enterprise, and private property." It carries advertisements for a book proving that the "Communist Conspiracy" is behind the Negro revolution in America.

The Review of the News is published from the same address as American Opinion, a substantial readership of which consists of members of the John Birch Society.

Richard Cotten's Conservative Viewpoint

Address: P.O. Box 1808
    Bakersfield, California
Newspaper: Bimonthly; $3.50 per 11 issues
Radio scripts: 6 days weekly; contributions of $10.00 per quarter
Circulation: Newspaper: 6,000-7,000
    Radio scripts: 12,000

Publication Started: 1963 (Newspaper recently renamed Richard Cotten's Proof Sheets)
Format: 6-page Newsletter
Issues Examined: September, 1965; radio scripts January 3, 4, 5, 28, 1966

    This newsletter is published by Richard B. Cotten, "spokesman for the Committee of Christian Laymen of Kern County, California." Cotten also publishes the scripts of his 15-minute daily radio program which is broadcast over 28 stations nationwide. These scripts bear the title Richard Cotten's Conservative Viewpoint.
    Mr. Cotten has declared that he is "wholly dedicated to exposing Socialism, Communism, one worldism, and any other form of Totalitarianism that is undermining OUR WAY OF LIFE. We are FOR individual responsibility; for a RETURN to constitutional government, for LESS centralization of power; FOR State's Rights, and we are FOR exposing the Federal Reserve."
    In his newsletter and radio scripts, Mr. Cotten discusses various national issues of concern to him. For example, in "Censorship" he writes at length about what he considers the FCC threat to the radio voice of the right wing. In "Racial Discrimination!" he discusses a United Nations document which deals with racial discrimination, especially anti-Semitism. Mr. Cotten opposes the convention established by this document, because he feels that it will promote the Zionist aspiration to one world government, and will cause anyone who objects to the document to be "smeared as anti-Semitic." In another article, Mr. Cotten deals with the Rhodesia issue, opposing the sanctions against Rhodesia and supporting the Smith government. In one radio script, he warns of the draining of the silver reserves and urges his listeners to save silver for the future. Two of the broadcasts are devoted to the denial of the charge that Mr. Cotten is anti-Semitic. He states: " . . . if I fight Socialism, Communism and the U.N., I end up in opposition to those Jews who defend those institutions. . . ." He further states that Christian Constitutionalists (which he terms those like himself) "recognize the right of any religious belief and . . . respect and protect the right of 'minorities' to hold their religious beliefs,

and . . . do not 'hate, despise or condemn.'"

One issue of this periodical also contains editorials by Westbrook Pegler and Strom Thurmond. Another contains a recommended reading list by Mr. Cotten.

Mr. Cotten was formerly a member of the John Birch Society. He expresses his approval of Reverend Billy James Hargis, Dr. Carl McIntyre, and Dan Smoot.

Editor's Response:

"I would suggest that your analysis insofar as our newspaper is concerned is correct, but by omitting our daily radio scripts (Richard Cotten's Conservative Viewpoint) you have overlooked our major task." (Radio scripts have since been considered and the content incorporated into summary.)

S.O.S.!!! U.S.A., Ship of State

Address: 18 Boardman Street
        Salem, Massachusetts
Monthly; No charge
Circulation: 1,000

Publication Started: 1956 (formerly Tribune of Enslaved Nations)
Format: 16-page Newsletter
Issues Examined: January, February, and October, 1966

S. O. S. U.S.A. Ship of State is published by the Anti-Communist Confederation of Polish Freedom Fighters consisting of 1,468 members, organized in 1953, and headed by Jozef Mlot-Mroz, a Polish immigrant who spent "22 months in Communist concentration camps." This strongly anti-Communist organization works for the "freedom of the Enslaved and Captive Nations," such as Poland, and tries to rescue America from Communism "before it is too late."

This publication contains many pictures of Polish Freedom Fighters participating in anti-Communist demonstrations, letters from readers concerning Communism, and various articles exposing the danger of Communism and directing readers to means of fighting Communism. It advocates the formation of anti-Communist crusades acquainted with "the tactics and strategy of underground warfare."

One article seeks to show specific ways in which America is a "Communist occupied country." For example, "in 1945, the Constitution was quietly replaced by the United Nations charter." It also gives the "red record" of Arthur Goldberg and Arthur Schlesinger. Another article describes the specific tortures endured by editor Mlot-Mroz in Communist prisons.

This periodical is not greatly concerned with the theoretical aspects of the battle between Communism and capitalism. Rather, it deals with practical matters such as Soviet strategy in World War III. Its concern is exclusively with the battle against Communism. If it mentions another issue, such as civil rights, it is only in connection with Communism. It has a slight religious aspect: it uses the Cross as a symbol and makes various other religious references.

The publication contains many illustrations, including photographs and anti-Communist cartoons. Some issues include a full page advertisement of the John Birch Society.

The October 1966 issue contains a one page laudatory article by Gerald L. K. Smith on the giant statue of Christ (7 stories high) at Eureka Springs, Arkansas, near which he and his wife expect to "be laid to rest" when their time on this earth has terminated. On the same page is an insert in large letters reading "The Jews created Communism." On another page is a photograph showing the editor counter-picketing in front of county jail (in opposition to pacifist pickets) and carrying a large sign reading "Communism is Jewish from Beginning to Finish. Fight Communism!"

Editor's Response:
"I do think that it is a fair, adequate and aptly worded characterization of my publication."

Tactics

Address: Anti-Communist Liaison, Inc.
P.O. Box 3541
Arlington, Virginia 22203
Monthly; $10.00 per year; single copes $1.00
Circulation: 1,050

Publication Started: 1964
Format: 4- to 8-page Newsletter
Issues Examined: September 20 and supplement, October 20 and supplement, and November 20, 1965

Edward Hunter, publisher-editor of Tactics, writes that the publication "is not a news bulletin and it does not seek to convert anyone. Tactics is designed for more or less knowledgeable persons who seek to use their influence to help maintain and expand American traditions and to help defeat Communism." Many of its articles deal with Communist infiltration of American institutions, and how to spot and counteract it. A statement in the September 20 issue, reflecting this concern, reads: "Failure to understand Communist tactics has led us and others time and again to rejoice over a victory when the Communists were busy using their defeat to put over their other objective, often the far more important one."

Articles cover a wide range of subjects, although limited to the general theme of Communist tactics and how to fight them. The September issue contains an article on the State Department case involving Otto Fred Otepka security chief, and colleagues of his, including John R. Norpel, Jr. Otepka was discharged after providing documentation to support statements made in reply to questions asked him by Senators in regard to accusations of lax security procedures. Senate indignation led to the suspension of his discharge, pending a hearing. Norpel and others were transferred away from security. Tactics commented on this matter as follows: "out of the Administration's woodwork came the same influences that divert or paralyze any government project once it threatens to really hurt the Communists." The September supplement dealt entirely with President Johnson's announcement to use the Pentagon computer system throughout government. Tactics pointed out that "computers can be employed properly as adjuncts for efficient procedure," but warned against attributing policy-making decisions to them, declaring this would constitute "a greater barrier than ever before to new thought, creativeness, initiative, or the discovery of any critical blunder, or, especially, perversion of national interests."

The October 20 issue contains a lengthy article on the Berkeley demonstrations. Tactics said: "The student riots, in which faculty members have collaborated . . . should have removed any doubts regarding the depth and scope of the pro-Communist infiltration into the American educational system."

The supplement to this issue is given over entirely to an analysis of negotiations with the Communists. It declares the Communists organize negotiations as a trap, pointing out: "American blood is flowing in Vietnam now as a consequence of two such lopsided conferences held with the Communists."

The November 20 issue contains what it calls a "propaganda analysis" of the New York Times, with reverence to the Berkeley demonstration. It declares the way the N.Y. Times covered such events was "helpful to subversives." The publication charges that N.Y. Times policy omits reference to Communist connections, although knowledge of it is necessary for an understanding of the news, while bringing in such rightist connections as membership in the John Birch Society repeatedly and unnecessarily.

Task Force

Address: Defenders of the American
         Constitution, Inc.
         Ormond Beach, Florida
Monthly; $5.00 per year
Circulation: 5,000

Publication Started: 1954
Format: 4-page Newsletter
Issues Examined: August and September, 1965

Task Force seeks "to defend the Constitution of the United States against all enemies, foreign or domestic." It bitterly opposes the tactics of limited war in Vietnam, "fought with no thought of winning," while Communist countries supply war material to the enemy. Task Force also opposes using the channels of the United Nations, stating that the Security Council "is always headed by a Communist."

Discussing domestic policy, Task Force attacks Executive Orders as undermining the Constitution and criticizes the voting-rights bill as establishing a federal dictatorship." It is also critical of the Supreme Court, on the grounds that it exceeds its Constitutional function, by CREATING legislation rather than INTERPRETING it.

Editor's Response:
No approval or disapproval expressed. Two statements of substance suggested as additions to the summary were incorporated in the text. Quotations from articles referring to an alleged coalition between U Thant and Martin Luther King and to advocacy of total war against Communism and opposition to any and all negotiations with Communists were crossed out and therefore, have been deleted from the summary.

Tocsin

Address: 515 East 10th Street
      Davis, California 95616
Biweekly; $10.00 per year
Circulation: 15,000

Publication Started: 1961
Format: 4- to 12-page Newsletter
Issues Examined: April 22, August 19, August 26, 1965; May 18, 1966

Tocsin was first subtitled, "The West's Leading Anti-Communist Weekly" and later, "The Weekly Intelligence Report." Tocsin's main focus is the bay area of California--Berkeley, Oakland and San Francisco. However, items of interest to other parts of the United States have been added increasingly. The journal utilizes photographs extensively. In recent issues, Tocsin keeps a close eye on the political activities on the Berkeley Campus of the University of California. The journal seeks to expose the activities of those involved in the Free Speech Movement, those involved in opposing the war in Vietnam, and those signing various left-wing petitions on the Berkeley Campus and elsewhere. Other articles report on how the "New Left" recruits boosters and activists, and how the May 2nd Movement started. Also discussed is a World Fellowship summer camp run by Willard Uphaus in New Hampshire.

Editor's Response:
"[The assistant] is to be commended for his objectivity and for abstracting the 'flavor.'"

The Top of the News

Address: Fulton Lewis, Productions
         Sheraton Park Hotel
         Washington, D.C. 20008
Weekly; $15.00 per year
Circulation: Not available for publication

Publication Started: 1959
Format: 4-page Newsletter
Issues Examined: August 16, 23, and 30; September 3, 1965

    The Top of the News is published weekly by Fulton Lewis, Productions. When started in July 1959 and until the time of his death in August 1966, the publication reprinted the scripts of five 15-minute newscasts by Fulton Lewis, Jr. The radio program has been taken over by Mr. Lewis' son, Fulton Lewis III and publication of the Newsletter is being continued.

    In his August 16 through 20, 1965 broadcasts Mr. Lewis discussed the riots in the Watts area of Los Angeles, California. He stated that "What happened in Los Angeles was not between Negroes and whites but among Negroes and Negroes. It was an insurrection against law enforcement . . . . " He also stated that the Negroes in Los Angeles have precisely identical opportunity for schooling, housing, and the use of public facilities as the whites. Finally, he spoke out against civil disobedience and the anti-poverty program, praising Senator Dirksen's opposition to the poverty program in its present form. Part of an address by Herbert V. Prochnow, President, First National Bank of Chicago, entitled "America's Strength--the Individual" also appears in this Top of the News issue.

    Fulton Lewis III substituted for his father during part of the week of August 23-27, 1965, speaking on the American Conservative Union, teen-age Republicans, the war in Vietnam, space achievements, the steel workers' strike, and the American Legion Convention. The remainder of Mr. Prochnow's address, "America's Strength--the Individual," is also printed in this issue.

    The August 30-September 3, 1965 issue of The Top of the News concentrates on the alleged "steamrolling" techniques used by the Administration and its supporters in getting President Johnson's Great Society program enacted. Finally, he discusses the attempt to repeal the section of the Taft-Hartley Act allowing state "right-to-work" laws. He gives arguments from both sides; he gives facts and figures favoring the repeal. This issue also contains a speech by Richard Nixon entitled "The Choice in Vietnam."

Editor's Response:
    "I have made only one minor correction."

The Truth about Communism

Address: 3400 West Michigan Street
       Milwaukee, Wisconsin 53208
Published six times during the school
   year
Circulation: 4,000

Publication Started: 1960
Format: 4-page Newsletter
Issues Examined: Nos. 26, 27, 28,
   and 29

   The Truth (about Communism), edited by the "Political Science Club," Marquette University High School, presents in-depth and closely-reasoned analyses of Communist activity. The issues reviewed all concentrate upon the external threat of Communism. This main topic is divided into several sub-topics, each of which serves as subject matter for one issue of The Truth. For example, issue No. 26 is entitled "A Psycho-Political Counterattack, Section II: Offensive Strategy." This issue argues that Americans must be capable of thinking offensively in our struggle with world Communism. Another issue, "Vietnam--Valiant Struggle for Freedom, Part I: A 'Persecution' Is Invented," argues that the clamor about Buddhist persecution under Diem is a contrived piece of Communist propaganda.
   Each issue of The Truth contains a summary of the content of the preceding issue, as well as a bibliography of source material.

Editor's Response:
   "Fine"

The Wanderer

Address: 128 East 10th Street
     St. Paul 1, Minnesota
Weekly; $5.00 per year
Circulation: 32,000

Publication Started: 1867 (from 1867
   to 1957 published in German; English publication began & ran concurrently with German to 1957, continues to date.)
Format: 8- to 10-page Newspaper
Issues Examined: October 21 and 28,
   November 4, 1965

   The Wanderer is a conservative, independent Catholic publication. The weekly newspaper contains news briefs and analyses, sydicated columnists, feature articles, regular religious features and a full page of editorials. For example, news coverage is presented in two lengthy regular features, "World Events of the Past Week," and "Events and Trends in the U.S."

-150-

In these features analyses are sometimes interspersed with factual presentations.

A feature entitled "Dateline: Hollywood" gives a Catholic censorial view of the happenings in the motion picture world. Other articles in The Wanderer concentrate on anti-Communist, anti-leftist topics and religious affairs, including such articles as "Commie Training School in Cuba," "disciple of 'Catholic' Worker First Arrested as Draft Card Destroyer," "Campus Communists--America's Time Bomb?", and "Warns of Concession on Birth Control." While editorials include "Towards a Red Takeover in the USA," "Attack from within," (concerning internal criticism of the Church by liberals), and "We Dare Call It Treason!", a few short articles on local affairs are usually included in The Wanderer.

In the issues reviewed, syndicated columns by Edith Kermit Roosevelt, William Buckley, Jr., Elizabeth Churchill Brown, and Robert Morris, conservative spokesmen, appear regularly. Feature articles include reports on the activities of the Ecumenical Council by Msgr. Ro G. Bandas, special Wanderer correspondent to the Second Vatican Council, and a page of articles entitled "Home and Fireside," discussing religious matters.

Editor's Response:
"OK"

The Weekly Crusader

Address: P.O. Box 977
       Tulsa, Oklahoma 74102
Weekly; $10.00 per year
Circulation: 5,000

Publication Started: 1960
Format: 8-page Newsletter
Issues Examined: July 30, August 6, 13, 20, and September 24, 1966

Christian Crusade publishes The Weekly Crusader as well as the Christian Crusade, a monthly magazine. The Weekly Crusader, like the Christian Crusade, presents a conservative and anti-Communist viewpoint. It deals with questions of domestic and foreign policy. Most issues generally center on one specific topic.

One issue focusing on Indonesia criticizes the State Department for recommending more military aid to Indonesia and points out that Sukarno has time and again proclaimed his country's friendship with Red China and Russia, publicly repudiated United States aid, and denounced U.S. foreign policy. "The inability of thinking members of Congress to eliminate aid to such sworn and dedicated enemies of America can happen only because of the deep sleep of apathy and complacency now being 'enjoyed' by a thoroughly brainwashed American public," the magazine asserts. Conversly, The Weekly Crusader criticizes America's lack of assistance to anti-Communists in foreign countries.

The magazine attacks America's lack of recognition of the Communist threat. In "The Anarcho-Communist Coalition," a reprint from the <u>Washington Report</u> (a publication of the American Security Council), it is argued that "it would be a mistake for Americans to dismiss the campus anarchists as a new species of crank . . . [because] the underlying philosophy of the anarcho-Communist coalition bears a resemblance to the philosophy enunciated by the Chinese Communists." It charges that U.S. Communists are also taking advantage of left-wing peace advocates for the purpose of furthering the goals of world Communism.

In other areas, an article attacks Justice Douglas' views on the relativity of truth, presenting a case for the employment of absolutes, in both intellectual and moral judgments, and stating that no comparative judgments can be made unless there are absolute standards. Regarding the race riots of Los Angeles, one issue states that "The Negro has been duped . . . by Communist agitators."

Editor's Response:
"It seems to me to be a fair summary."

Wire Magazine

Address: 549 Masten Avenue
         Buffalo, New York 14209
Monthly; $2.40 per year
Circulation: 3,850

Publication Started: 1963
Format: Small size, 20-page Magazine
Issues Examined: October, December, 1965; January, February, 1966

<u>Wire Magazine</u> is mainly directed in opposition to the civil rights movement because the editors believe that it is part of the Communist conspiracy. "Communism is treason" is one of their slogans. The magazine believes that "the Negro needs white help. He must be given it. But it must be help built on law and order and both personal and race responsibility." The latter sentence reflects a recurring theme in <u>Wire</u>'s articles. All the major civil rights organizations such as the NAACP, CORE and SNCC are condemned as being Communist inspired. Dr. Martin Luther King is described as being "the most dangerous pro-Communist agitator in America today," and is blamed as "directly or indirectly responsible for the chaos, anarchy, insurrection, and rebellion brought about through demonstrations and rioting throughout the U.S." The policy of the magazine toward civil rights and the Negro is, rather than rioting, the Negro should work to get ahead for himself. "The fact that Negroes are on the bottom of the totem pole as far as our economy, is due to their own folly." The publication points to a Negro editor, George Schuyler, as believing that the "Negro

Americans, in their own interests, should be conservatives rather than radicals."

The concern of the magazine for the Communist inspiration of the civil rights movement is major; however, the editors see other organizations as being just as infiltrated. For example: they describe the National Council of Churches as having "promoted liberal, left-wing causes"; the U.N. is described as "but a Trojan-horse instrument of Soviet foreign policy"; and "the pro-Communist conspiracy has made a desperate attempt to secure high school students . . . under the guise that the students are working for civil rights."

Each issue of the magazine examined contains short news articles and editorials. Some of these are reprinted from other publications.

Editor's Response:

" . . . Negro clergy are frauds for they preach a foreign doctrine of the Bible and have joined with unconverted left-wing white clergy to use racial agitation to get publicity and money. These hypocrites condem [sic] school systems charging racial unbalance of a school if it has more Negroes than white students while at the same time the Negro and white clergy maintain segregated congregations and church schools and colleges in the North as well as in the South.

"Communism and racial agitation is Treason. 'Lets Fight It With Common Sense and Education.'"

The editor expressed no disapproval.

The Woman Constitutionalist

Address: 310 West Robb Street
P.O. Box 220
Summit, Mississippi
Monthly; $1.00 per year
Circulation: 9,000

Publication Started: 1964
Format: 8-page tabloid Newspaper
Issues Examined: November 6, December 4, 1965; January 1, February 5, 1966

The Woman Constitutionalist is the official organ of Women for Constitutional Government, "a non-political organization of concerned women." They believe in "a constitutional government and see each day this republic being systematically destroyed by satanic forces of men and women fully dedicated to the task of destroying Christian America."

The greatest emphasis of The Woman Constitutionalist is on return to the kind of government established by the Constitution. A typical statement is this: "Congress must reassert its constitutional role if fiscal soundness is to be restored." The Woman Constitutionalist sees expansion of the functions of Federal government as the greatest threat to Constitutional government, The Great Society representing this expansion at its greatest.

This monthly emphasizes restoration of freedom and of states' rights. It advocates a Liberty amendment "which would force the government out of competition with private enterprise and eventually repeal the sixteenth amendment."

The Woman Constitutionalist opposes such programs as social security, medicare, and the war on poverty. It repeatedly expresses fears about Federal spending. It is against civil rights movements, also, although it expresses very little specifically anti-Negro sentiment.

With regard to foreign policy, The Woman Constitutionalist vigorously opposes Communism and the United Nations, which commits us to "World Government." The United Nations issue takes a large proportion of space in this publication. The Woman Constitutionalist is for "victory" in Vietnam, and it opposes the sanctions against Rhodesia.

There is a moralistic tone to much of what is said in this publication. There are frequent references to God, honor, and the Bible.

ALPHABETICAL INDEX TO TITLES

This Index presents all titles in alphabetical order and gives first a chapter number reference and then a page reference. The chapter number reference is helpful in categorizing the publication per the editor's criteria.

For ready reference a list of chapter numbers and titles is presented here:

Chapter	Title
1	Civil Rights and Negro
2	Left of Center
3	Miscellaneous
4	Pacifist
5	Race-Oriented
6	Right of Center

Activist	2	13	The Citizen	5	90
ADA Legislative News-			Civil Liberties	3	62
letter	2	14	CNVA Bulletin	4	80
ADA World	1	15	Common Sense	5	91
Age of Reason	3	58	CORE-lator	1	1
American Atheist: A			Councilor	5	92
Voice of Reason	3	58	Crisis	1	1
American Dialog	2	15	Cross and the Flag	5	93
American Flag Com-			Dan Smoot Report	6	110
mittee Newsletter	6	101	Dart Bulletin	6	111
American Mercury	6	102	Despite Everything	2	22
American Opinion	6	103	Destiny	3	63
American Socialist	2	16	Dissent	2	23
American-Soviet Facts			Economic Council Letter	6	112
(see Facts)	2	24	Fact Finder	6	112
America's Future	6	104	Facts	2	24
Antithesis	2	17	Facts for Freedom (see		
Between the Lines	3	59	In a Nutshell)	2	122
Bulletin of International			FCNL Washington News-		
Socialism	2	19	letter	3	64
Capital Voice	6	105	Federalist	3	64
Capsule News	3	60	Fellowship	4	80
Catholic Worker	2	20	Firing Line	6	113
Challenge-Desafio	2	21	Four Lights	4	82
Christian Anti-Commun-			Free Enterprise	6	115
ist Crusade	6	106	Free Student	2	25
Christian Beacon	6	107	Freedom Talks	6	128
Christian Crusade	6	107	Freedom's Facts	6	113
Christian Economics	6	108	Freedom's Way	6	114
Church and State	3	61	Freedomways	1	2
			Freeman	6	115

-155-

Title	Col	Page
Frontier	2	26
Gospel Truth	6	116
Grass Roots	6	117
Greater Nebraskan	6	118
Hammer and Steel Newsletter	2	27
Heads Up	6	119
Herald of Freedom	6	120
Human Events	6	120
I. F. Stone's Weekly	2	28
Imua Spotlight	6	121
In a Nutshell	6	122
The Independent	3	65
Independent American	6	123
Industrial Worker	2	29
Inform-National Reports	6	124
Insurgent	2	29
Intercollegiate Review	3	67
International Socialist Review	2	30
Interracial Review	1	3
Kansas Free Lance	6	125
Keeping the Record Straight	6	126
Left and Right	3	68
Liberation	2	31
Liberator	1	4
Liberty Letter	6	127
Life Lines	6	128
Manion Forum	6	129
The Militant	2	32
Mindszenty Report	6	130
Minority of One	3	69
Minute Women	6	130
Modern Age	6	131
Monthly Review	2	34
Movement	1	5
Muhammad Speaks	1	6
National Christian News	5	94
National Chronicle	5	95
National Forecast	6	132
National Guardian	2	35
National Program Letter	6	133
National Renaissance Bulletin	5	96
New America	2	37
New Guard	6	133
New Individualist Review	6	134
New Leader	3	71
New Politics	2	39
New South	1	7
New University Thought	3	72
New World Review	2	40
News and Letters	2	42
News and Views	6	136
News Notes (of the Central Committee for Conscientious Objectors)	4	82
The Objectivist	6	136
On Target	6	138
Our American Heritage Committee News Bulletin	6	139
Partisan	2	43
Peace	4	83
Peace Action	4	84
Peacemaker	4	84
People's World	2	43
Petal Paper	1	9
Pilgrim Torch	5	97
The Plain Truth	6	140
Political Affairs	2	44
Progressive	2	46
Progressive Labor	2	47
Rampart Journal of Individualistic Thought	6	141
Ramparts	3	73
Rank and File	6	142
Realist	3	74
Reporter for Conscience' Sake	4	85
Review of the News	6	143
Richard Cotten's Conservative Viewpoint	6	144
Rights	3	75
Rockwell Report	5	97
Sane World	4	86
SCLC Newsletter	1	9
SDS Bulletin	2	48

Social Questions Bulletin	3	76
SOS!!! U.S.A. Ship of State	6	145
Southern Courier	1	10
Southern Patriot	1	11
Spark-Chispa	2	48
Spartacist	2	49
Stormtrooper	5	98
Student Peace Union Bulletin	4	86
Studies on the Left	2	50
Tactics	6	146
Task Force	6	147
Thunderbolt	5	98
Tocsin	6	148
Top of the News	6	149
Towards Anarchism	3	77
The Truth About Communism	6	150
Truth Seeker	5	99
Viet Report	2	51
The Voice	1	11
The Wanderer	6	150
War/Peace Report	4	87
WRL News	4	88
Washington Observer Newsletter (see American Mercury)	6	102
WCLC Newsletter	1	12
Weekly Crusader	6	151
Weekly People	2	53
Western Socialist	2	54
White American	5	99
William Winter Comments	3	73
Wire Magazine	6	152
Woman Constitutionalist	6	153
The Worker	2	55
Workers' World	2	56
World News and Comments	3	78
Young Socialist	2	56

Supplement

to

FROM RADICAL LEFT TO EXTREME RIGHT

Showing Changes Reported
Up to August 1, 1967

ROBERT H. MULLER
Editor

After the publication FROM RADICAL LEFT TO EXTREME RIGHT came off the press, a request was sent to all the periodicals listed to bring the information up to date. Of the 162 periodicals listed, 140 responded. Of the 140, 14 have ceased publication or moved without leaving a forwarding address. Of the 22 that failed to respond, 11 seemed still to be published according to a check made against recent receipts in the University of Michigan Library. The other 11 may also have ceased publication.

Most of the changes were in the address, frequency, circulation, price of subscription, and format.

THE ACTIVIST
    Circulation: 2,500
AMERICAN ATHEIST
    Publication discontinued as of January, 1966.
AMERICAN DIALOG
    No response. Vol. 4, No. 1, 1967 received.
AMERICAN FLAG COMMITTEE NEWSLETTER
    Format: 4-page Newsletter, Photo-offset
AMERICAN SOCIALIST
    Moved and left no address.
AMERICA'S FUTURE
    Address: Add Zip Code #10802
    Complimentary subscriptions available to public and school libraries and and also to bona fide college students.
ANTITHESIS
    Moved and left no address.
BULLETIN OF INTERNATIONAL SOCIALISM
    Format: 4-page printed Newspaper
CAPITAL VOICE
    Address: 1501 Farragut Street, N.W.
CAPSULE NEWS
    Address: Add Zip Code #22201
    Publication Started: 1955
    Format: 8-page Newsletter

CATHOLIC WORKER
    Circulation: 90,000
CHRISTIAN BEACON
    Address: Add Zip Code #08108
    Circulation: 80,000
CHRISTIAN CRUSADE
    Circulation: 90,000
CHRISTIAN ECONOMICS
    Contributions of $2.00 are solicited once or twice a year.
    Circulation: 215,000
    Publication Started: 1950
CHURCH AND STATE
    Circulation: 150,000
CITIZEN
    No response. Vol. 11, No. 9, June 1967 received.
CIVIL LIBERTIES
    Circulation: 100,000
    Format: 6- to 8-page tabloid
CNVA BULLETIN
    Publication discontinued.
CORE-lator
    Publication discontinued.
THE CRISIS
    No response.
DAN SMOOT REPORT
    Circulation: 31,000
DART BULLETIN
    Format: 4-,6-, or 8-page mimeographed Newsletter
DESPITE EVERYTHING QUARTERLY
    16- to 40-page lithographed Magazine
DISSENT
    No response. May 1967 issue received.
FEDERALIST
    Format: 8- to 12-page Newsletter
FELLOWSHIP
    Address: Add Zip Code #10960
FREE ENTERPRISE
    Format: 8-page tabloid Newspaper
FREE STUDENT
    Address unknown.
FREEDOM'S WAY
    No response. Vol. 4, No. 1, April, 1967 received.
FREEDOMWAYS
    Format: 6" x 9", 100- to 200-page Magazine
FRONTIER
    No response. Vol. 18, No. 3, 1967 received.
GRASS ROOTS
    Circulation: National
    Format: 16-page mimeographed Journal
THE GREATER NEBRASKAN
    Address: Add Zip Code #68105

HEADS UP
    No response.
I.F. STONE'S WEEKLY
    Circulation: 32,000
    Publication Started: January 1953
IMUA SPOTLIGHT
    Monthly.
    Executive Vice-President of the Hawaii Foundation for American Freedoms, Inc. requests this periodical to be classified in the "Miscellaneous" category.
INDEPENDENT AMERICAN
    Format: 8-page Newspaper
INDUSTRIAL WORKER
    $2.00 per year
    Format: 8-page tabloid
INSURGENT
    Moved and left no address.
INTERCOLLEGIATE REVIEW
    Format: 48- to 60-page Magazine
INTERNATIONAL SOCIALIST REVIEW
    Address: 873 Broadway
             New York, New York 10003
    Circulation: 4,000
    Format: 48- to 64-page Magazine
INTERRACIAL REVIEW
    No response.
KANSAS FREE LANCE
    Bimonthly; $5.00 per year
LEFT AND RIGHT
    No response.
LIBERATION
    Address: Add Zip Code #10038
    Format: 40- to 48-page Magazine
LIBERATOR
    No response. Vol. 7, No. 4, April 1967 received.
LIBERTY LETTER
    $2.00
LIFE LINES
    Three times per week; $5.00 per year
    Circulation: 10,000
    Publication Started: September 1959
MINUTE WOMEN
    Monthly (Newsletter received bimonthly, California Bulletin received on alternate months); $5.00 per year
MONTHLY REVIEW
    Monthly (11 issues per year, including a double summer issue); $6.00 per year
MOVEMENT
    No response. Vol. 3, No. 5, May 1967 received.

MUHAMMAD SPEAKS
    No response.
NATIONAL CHRISTIAN NEWS
    No response. Vol. 5, No. 1, 1967 received.
NATIONAL FORECAST
    Publication discontinued.
NATIONAL GUARDIAN
    Format: 12- or 16-page tabloid Newspaper
NATIONAL PROGRAM LETTER
    $5.00 per year
NATIONAL RENAISSANCE BULLETIN
    Every two months
    Circulation: 3,000
    Publication Started: January 1949
    Format: 7-1/2" x 11" Newsletter, 8- to 12-pages
NEW INDIVIDUALIST REVIEW
    Address: Add Zip Code #60637
    Omit student rate
NEW LEADER
    Address: American Labor Conference on International Affairs
         212 Fifth Avenue
         New York, New York 10010
    Omit "irregular"
    Format: 31- to 61-page Magazine
NEW POLITICS
    No response.
NEW SOUTH
    Quarterly; $3.00 per ear
    Circulation: 2,150
    Format: 70- to 100-page Magazine
NEW UNIVERSITY THOUGHT
    $5.00 per year
    Format: Small size, 80-page Magazine
NEWS AND LETTERS
    Address: 415 Brainard
         Detroit, Michigan 48201
NEWS NOTES (of the Central Committee for Conscientious Objectors)
    Circulation: 13,500
OBJECTIVIST NEWSLETTER
    Address: The Objectivist, Inc.
         Empire State Building - LL26
         350 Fifth Avenue
         New York, New York 10001
ON TARGET
    No response. May 1, 1967 received.
PARTISAN
    Circulation: 4,000
PEOPLE'S WORLD
    Circulation: 7,228

PETAL PAPER
    Circulation: 2,300
PILGRIM TORCH
    Quarterly
    Circulation: 80,000
PLAIN TRUTH
    Circulation: 970,000
POLITICAL AFFAIRS
    Address: 799 Broadway, Room 618
              New York, New York 10003
PROGRESSIVE
    No response. Vol. 31, No. 7, July 1967 received.
PROGRESSIVE LABOR
    Circulation: 10,000
    Format: 140-page Magazine
RAMPART JOURNAL OF INDIVIDUALIST THOUGHT
    Circulation: 900 total, 853 paid
RAMPARTS
    Address: Add Zip Code #94133
    $8.50 per year
    Circulation: 228,000
    Format: 60-page Magazine
RANK AND FILE
    No response.
REALIST
    Monthly, except for January and July
    Circulation: 100,000
    Format: 24-page Magazine
RICHARD COTTEN'S CONSERVATIVE VIEWPOINT
    "Proof Sheet" is no longer being published.
RIGHTS
    Address: Add Zip Code #10001
ROCKWELL REPORT
    Publication discontinued. Will be replaced by
    THE WHITE AMERICAN, tentatively, as of September
    1967, which will be monthly, at 15¢ per issue.
SANE WORLD
    Address: 381 Park Avenue South
              New York, New York 10016
    Circulation: 22,000
SCLC NEWSLETTER
    Publication discontinued.
SDS BULLETIN
    No response.
SOCIAL QUESTIONS BULLETIN
    Format: 4-page Newsletter
S.O.S.!!! U.S.A., SHIP OF STATE
    No response.
SOUTHERN COURIER
    $3.50 per year in South
SPARK - CHIPSA
    No response. Vol. 3, No. 3, 1967 received.

SPARTACIST
    Circulation: 10,000
STUDENT PEACE UNION BULLETIN
    Publication discontinued.
THUNDERBOLT
    Address: P.O. Box 6263
                  Savannah, Georgia 31405
    Publication is regular
TOCSIN
    Publication discontinued.
TOP OF THE NEWS
    Address: The National Press Building
                  14th and F Streets, N.W.
                  Washington, D.C. 20004
TOWARDS ANARCHISM
    Address unknown.
TRUTH SEEKER
    Address: Add Zip Code #92112
VIET-REPORT
    Nine times per year
VOICE
    Publication discontinued. There is another publication: SNCC NEWSLETTER, at the same address, which costs $2.00 per year and which is issued monthly.
WAR/PEACE REPORT
    U.S. Student rate, $3.50
WCLC NEWSLETTER
    No response.
WHITE AMERICAN
    No response.
WIRE MAGAZINE
    Address: 494 Masten Avenue
                  Buffalo, New York 14209
    Format: Small size, 16-page Magazine
WOMAN CONSTITUTIONALIST
    $2.00 per year
    Circulation: 10,000
WORKERS WORLD
    Format: 4-page tabloid Newspaper until Nov. 8, 1966, and thereafter 8-pages
WORLD NEWS AND COMMENTS
    Name changed to WILLIAM WINTER COMMENTS, the original name.
    Address: Sausalito
    Circulation: 3,000
YOUNG SOCIALIST
    Monthly (bi-monthly in the summer, giving a total of 11 issues a year); $1.25 per year

ERRATA

Chiefly, Corrections of Minor Errors
in Printing and Spelling

Second Supplement to

FROM RADICAL LEFT TO EXTREME RIGHT

ROBERT H. MULLER
Editor

Page iii.   "...International" should read "International)".

Page iv.   "World News and Comments (now...)" should be omitted. The title is simply "William Winter Comments".

Page vi.   "(Conservative employee magazine)" should read "(Conservative Employee Magazine)".

Page xi.   Paragraph 2. Line 9.
            "Party, and; had" should read "Party; and had".

Page xii.   Within the quote. Line 3.
            "idealogical" should read "ideological".

Page xvii. Paragraph 2. Line 11.
            "typing" should read "tying".

Page 1.   CORE-lator. Paragraph 1. Line 3.
            "non-violent" should read "nonviolent".

Page 3.   Interracial Review.
            Publication discontinued until 1968.

Page 5.   The Movement. Data.
            Monthly; $2.00 per year
            Circulation: 6,000
            Format: 12-page tabloid Newspaper.

Page 9.   The Petal Paper. Paragraph 3. Lines 5 and 7.
            "man" should read "many" and "throughou" should read "throughout".

Page 22.   Paragraph 1. Lines 2 and 3.
            "be Movement" should read "the Movement".
            "Civil Rights Movement" should read "civil rights movement".
            "Now, the meaning insensibly broadens, as it should)." should be omitted.

-164-

Page 24.   Lines 14 and 15.
           The quotation mark (") at the end of line 14
              should be omitted.
           A quotation mark (") should precede '"US and
              USSR See Gains in Settling UN Dispute"'.

Page 25.   Line 4.
           A quotation mark (") should follow the end
              of the first sentence: 'the people of
              Vietnam."'

Page 31.   Paragraph 1. Line 2.
           "reconstitueted" should read "reconstituted".

Page 32.   Paragraph 2. Line 2.
           "naintains" should read "maintains".

Page 40.   Paragraph 2. Line 2.
           "expose" should read "exposé".

Page 48.   <u>SDS Bulletin</u>. Paragraph 2. Line 3.
           "$5.00" should read "$10.00".

Page 59.   Paragraph 3. Line 4.
           "degregationists" should read "segregationists".

Page 62.   Paragraph 2. Line 5.
           "trmendous" should read "tremendous".

Page 67.   Paragraph 1. Line 2.
           Quotation marks (") should follow 'free
              society",'.

Page 72.   Paragraph 3. Last line.
           A period should occur at the end of the line.

Page 78.   Data. Address information.
           "Sausolito" should read "Sausalito".

Page 82.   Line 6.
           "March" should read "march".

Page 83.   <u>Peace</u>. Data.
           Format: Replace "small size Magazine with
              approximately 28 pages" with "8- to 12-page
              Newsletter".

Page 86.   Paragraph 2. Line 8.
           "Sane" should read "<u>Sane World</u>".

-165-

Page 94.   Paragraph 4. Lines 3 and 5.
"world council of churches" should read "World Council of Churches".
"It is pro-Nazi claiming" should read "It is pro-Nazi, claiming".

Page 99.   Data. Address information for <u>The White American</u>.
"8399" should read "8299".

Page 102. Paragraph 5. Line 7.
"-hot-bed" should read "hot-bed".

Page 107. Both titles.
"CHRISTIAN BEACON" should read "Christian Beacon".
"CHRISTIAN CRUSADE" should read "Christian Crusade".

Page 113. The entry on <u>Free Enterprise</u> should be inserted between <u>Firing Line</u> and <u>Freedom's Facts</u>, in order to retain alphabetical order.

Page 114. <u>Freedom's Way</u>. Data.
Circulation: "164" should read "152".

Page 115. <u>Free Enterprise</u> should be transferred to Page 13.

Page 116. <u>The Gospel Truth</u>. Paragraph 1. Line 1.
Quotation marks (") should precede '"is a publication'.

Page 125. <u>The Kansas Free Lance</u>. Paragraph 1. Line 3.
A quotation mark (") should precede '"the'.

Page 126. Paragraph 4. Line 5.
"Miss" should be replaced by "Edith".

Page 129. Paragraph 2. Line 1.
"Fred Schlafly an Illinois" should read "Fred Schlafly, an Illinois".

Page 132. <u>National Forecast</u>. Paragraph 1. Line 5.
The quotation mark (") following 'government"' should be omitted.

Page 134. Paragraph 1. Line 3.
"issues oriented" should read "issue-oriented".
"while" should read "While".

-166-

Page 138.   Paragraph 3. Line 5.
            "<u>physical force (by initiating</u>" should read
            "<u>physical force</u> (by initiating".
            The quotation mark (') preceding "'good"
               should be omitted.

Page 138.   <u>On Target</u>.
            Temporarily discontinued.

Page 141.   <u>Rampart Journal of Individual Thought</u>.
            The title should read "Rampart Journal
               of Individual<u>ist</u> Thought".

Page 156.   "Rampart Journal of Individualistic
               Thought" should read "Rampart
               Journal of Individualist Thought".

Page 157.   "World News and Comments" should be omitted.

-167-